THE STORM OF PROGRESS

THE STORM OF PROGRESS

Climate Change, AI, and the Roots of Our Dangerous Ethical Myopia

WADE ROWLAND

Edited by Kaiya Smith Blackburn
Index: Benjamin Bush Anderson
Proofread by Edward He
Cover design: Debbie Geltner
Cover background image: Freepik.com
Author photo: Christine Collie Rowland

Library and Archives Canada Cataloguing in Publication
Title: The storm of progress: climate change, AI, and the roots of our dangerous ethical myopia / Wade Rowland.
Names: Rowland, Wade, author.
Description: "An LLP singles title." | Includes index.
Identifiers: Canadiana (print) 20230506194 | Canadiana (ebook) 20230506240 | ISBN 9781773901497 (softcover) | ISBN 9781773901503 (PDF) | ISBN 9781773901510 (EPUB)
Subjects: LCSH: Artificial intelligence—Moral and ethical aspects. | LCSH: Artificial intelligence—Social aspects. | LCSH: Computers and civilization. | LCSH: Climatic changes—Effect of human beings on. | LCSH: Sustainability. | LCSH: Social responsibility of business.
Classification: LCC Q334.7 .R69 2024 | DDC 006.301—dc23

Printed and bound in Canada.

The publisher gratefully acknowledges the support of the Government of Canada through the Canada Council for the Arts, the Canada Book Fund, and of the Government of Quebec through the Société de développement des entreprises culturelles (SODEC).

Linda Leith Publishing
Montreal
www.lindaleith.com

Books by Wade Rowland

Morality By Design: Technology's Challenge to Human Values
Canada Lives Here: The Case for Public Broadcasting
Greed, Inc.: Why Corporations Rule Our World
Galileo's Mistake: The Archeology of a Myth
Ockham's Razor: A Season in France in Search of Meaning
Spirit of the Web: The Age of Information from Telegraph to Internet
The Plot to Save the World: The Life and Times of
the Stockholm Conference on the Human Environment

Two things fill the mind with ever new and increasing admiration and reverence, the more often and more steadily one reflects on them: the starry heavens above me and the moral law within me.

—Immanuel Kant

So many people today—and even professional scientists—seem to me to be like somebody who has seen thousands of trees but has never seen a forest. A knowledge of the historical and philosophical background gives that kind of independence from prejudices of his generation from which most scientists are suffering. This independence created by philosophical insight is—in my opinion—the mark of distinction between a mere artisan or specialist and a real seeker after truth.

—Albert Einstein

Contents

Preface

This book takes the form of a series of interconnected essays inquiring into a central issue. That issue is the threat posed by modern technologies to the habitability of our planet and the future of its human population. (You will find that my definition of technology is somewhat broader than is the usual case.) The essays draw on material I have published elsewhere in other forms over a long career in journalism and academia. I am grateful to Trent University for having welcomed me back to the academic fold when journalism was no longer providing the answers I sought, and to York University in Toronto for the privilege of being able to develop my thinking on the issue in conversation over a decade and a half with colleagues and students.

Much of the first half of the book is devoted to placing our current existential crises in their historic context; to looking critically into the ideas that shaped Western societies in the wake of the momentous era of intellectual ferment called the Enlightenment. Western civilization as it was shaped by Enlightenment philosophers and their ideas bequeathed not only astonishing prosperity and unprecedented human lifespans, but also the current crisis of climate change, and the looming threats posed by unregulated artificial intelligence, and nuclear warfare. This book asks why, given the now-manifest error of our ways, we made the choices we did. It contends that an important part of the answer has to do with a dwindling ability to think clearly about ethics and values in the face of the undeniable successes of our scientistic worldview, which today defines everything from biology and anthropology to cosmology. I propose a relatively new approach to the subject of value going forward, one known formally as critical moral realism, but which also fits the definition of common sense. I am happy to be able to report that a trend has developed in recent decades that gives cause for hope that we will one day soon be able to think more clearly and rationally in dealing with economic development, technology, and other areas of our shared existence on this planet that demand an interaction of fact and values in making sustainable, common-sense choices.

I would like to acknowledge the enthusiastic support given to this project by my publisher, Linda Leith, and the astute editorial suggestions made by my editor Kaiya Smith Blackburn.

1. Prologue

Half a century ago, a book called *Only One Earth* was published under the sponsorship of the inaugural United Nations Conference on the Human Environment. It was intended to raise the public profile of an emerging global crisis, and to focus attention on the first concerted attempt by the global community of nations to find solutions. It contained a distillation of hundreds of scientific reports, compiling the views and opinions of more than seventy scientists and intellectuals from around the world. This may sound like a recipe for literary disaster, but the book became an international bestseller, thanks to the writing and editing abilities of its two authors-of-record: the British economist Barbara Ward, and the Franco-American scientist and philosopher René Dubos. Here is how the book opens:

> Man inhabits two worlds. One is the natural world of plants and animals, of soils and airs and waters which preceded him by billions of years and of which he is a part. The other is the world of social institutions and artifacts he builds for himself, using his tools and engines, his science and his dreams to fashion an environment obedient to human purpose and direction.

And here is how it ends:

> Alone in space, alone in its life-supporting systems, powered by inconceivable energies, mediating them to us through the most delicate adjustments,

> wayward, unlikely, unpredictable, but nourishing, enlivening and enriching in the largest degree—is this not a precious home for all of us earthlings? Is it not worth our love? Does it not deserve all the inventiveness and courage and generosity of which we are capable to preserve it from degradation and destruction and, by doing so, secure our own survival?

In the intervening 280 pages, the authors support in great depth and detail their assertion that:

> As we enter the last decades of the 20th century … something fundamental and possibly irrevocable is happening to man's relations with both his [natural and social] worlds. Technical innovation undertaken in the cause of improving the quality of human existence has taken us to the point where our interventions in the natural order may be creating conditions entirely hostile to human well-being. And our social institutions [seem] incapable of containing and directing this vast technical momentum.[1]

As a young newspaper reporter and one of only a handful colleagues, worldwide, working a brand-new beat focusing on environmental issues, I travelled to Stockholm in the summer of 1972 to research a book on environmental diplomacy as it had been developing around the ground-breaking UN conference.

At the opening ceremonies I listened in a gilded hall crowded with diplomats and journalists as the great maritime explorer Jacques Cousteau reported that, in twenty years of roaming the seas of the world, he had witnessed a general decline in marine life of between thirty and fifty percent, because of pollution.

U Thant, the UN Secretary-General who had overseen five years of conference preparations, noted that worldwide fossil fuel energy demands were on an upward trajectory leading to an "increase in excess, unabsorbed carbon dioxide [which] could have a catastrophic warming effect, melting the polar ice, changing the marine environment and creating flooding on a global scale."[2] The word used by organizers of

---

1 Barbara Ward and René Dubos, *Only One Earth: The Care and Maintenance of a Small Planet* (New York: Penguin Books, 1972).

2 Wade Rowland, *The Plot to Save the World: The Life and Times of the Stockholm Conference on the Human Environment* (Toronto: Clarke, Irwin & Co., 1973). When the conference opened, U Thant had been succeeded by Kurt Waldheim.

the Stockholm conference to describe the problems of global warming, overpopulation, resource depletion, fragile food supplies, and pollution was "urgent." That was in 1972.

There has been a significant increase in public awareness of environmental issues over the past five decades. Today, almost any political jurisdiction of any size anywhere in the world has a ministry or secretariat of the environment or some equivalent authority. Prior to Stockholm, there were none. Today, every literate child knows the basic narrative of the interconnectedness and interdependence within planetary ecosystems. We take reusable bags to the grocery store and put our plastic, glass, and paper out for recycling on garbage day. Major resource, industrial, and commercial developments now require environmental certification almost everywhere in the world. Industrial pollution, where it is visible, is no longer tolerated as an unavoidable by-product of wealth-generation and job-creation. Toxic chemicals such as DDT and ozone-depleting refrigerants have been banned under international treaties. Great strides have been taken in sustainable energy technologies.

But for all this progress, what we now refer to as the global sustainability crisis has grown much more serious by almost every objective measurement. The sheer scale of environmental, social, and economic disaster confronting the world today is unprecedented—almost unimaginable.

The situation recalls the poignant reflections of philosopher Walter Benjamin, penned as the world plunged into the second global war in a generation:

> A Klee painting named *Angelus Novus* shows an angel looking as though he is about to move away from something he is fixedly contemplating. His eyes are staring, his mouth is open, his wings are spread. This is how one pictures the angel of history. His face is turned toward the past. Where we perceive a chain of events, he sees one single catastrophe which keeps piling wreckage upon wreckage and hurls it in front of his feet. The angel would like to stay, awaken the dead, and make whole what has been smashed. But a storm is blowing in from Paradise; it has got caught in his wings with such violence that the angel can no longer close them. This storm irresistibly propels him into the future to which his back is turned, while the pile of debris before him grows skyward. This storm is what we call progress.[3]

---

[3] Walter Benjamin, "On the Concept of History," Simon Fraser University, June 18, 2023, https://www.sfu.ca/~andrewf/CONCEPT2.html.

Equipped with undeniable evidence that we have somehow taken the wrong path in our pursuit of what has long been called "progress," we steadfastly cling to the very policies, institutions, and ideas that have led us to our current condition. Our faith in the redemptive mission of science seems only slightly shaken—in some quarters, not at all.

Technology, we seem to believe, is destiny, and with its help we are fated to return to Eden, if not on this planet, then on some other. Artificial intelligence and machine learning researchers are engineering and releasing products that, while promising to assist human efforts in almost every arena of endeavour, also promise to produce the kinds of unintended consequences economists call "externalities," the unwanted and sometimes disastrous by-products of industrial development usually left to society to clean up. Early in 2023, a host of highly respected AI researchers and entrepreneurs asked some pointed moral questions in an open letter calling for an immediate moratorium on the galloping development of artificial general intelligence products like ChatGPT, developed by the start-up OpenAI:

> Contemporary AI systems are now becoming human-competitive at general tasks, and we must ask ourselves: *Should* we let machines flood our information channels with propaganda and untruth? *Should* we automate away all the jobs, including the fulfilling ones? *Should* we develop nonhuman minds that might eventually outnumber, outsmart, obsolete and replace us? *Should* we risk loss of control of our civilization? Such decisions must not be delegated to unelected tech leaders. Powerful AI systems should be developed only once we are confident that their effects will be positive and their risks will be manageable.[4]

Large language models (LLMS) like ChatGPT are initially trained by exposing them to vast amounts of text scaped from the internet and can converse knowledgeably with humans on almost any topic. This makes them very useful for a wide range of applications from medical and pharmaceutical research to legal opinions. The potential for this kind of self-instructing machine intelligence seems virtually unlimited. Indeed, a small but significant number of experts in the field see a future in which out-of-control, super-intelligent AI threatens the very existence of humanity. Philosopher and AI pioneer Norbert Weiner warned in 1960 that machines that can teach themselves could develop novel strategies and behaviours at speeds far beyond human capacity. There would be no

---

4 Future of Life Institute, "Pause Giant AI Experiments: An Open Letter" (futureoflife.org, March 22, 2023).

guarantee that those strategies and behaviours would conform to human intentions. He used the German poet Goethe's fable of the sorcerer's apprentice to illustrate: a trainee sorcerer is instructed by its master to fetch water for a bath, but the sorcerer is unable to get the trainee to stop when the tub is full. Not having the common sense to see its job is complete, it goes on fetching pail after pail and floods the room.[5]

In *The Age of AI* by former US Secretary of State Henry Kissinger, former Google CEO Eric Schmidt, and Daniel Huttenlocher, dean of MIT's Schwarzman College of Computing, the authors observe:

> We are entering an era in which AI—a human creation—is increasingly entrusted with tasks that previously would have been performed, or attempted, by human minds. As AI executes these tasks, producing results approximating and sometimes surpassing those of human intelligence, it challenges a defining attribute of what it means to be human."

They point out that:

> The last time human consciousness was changed significantly—the Enlightenment—the transformation occurred because new technology engendered new philosophical insights, which, in turn, were spread by the technology (in the form of the printing press). In our period, new technology has been developed, but remains in need of a guiding philosophy.[6]

As we'll see, the Enlightenment transformation involved a movement away from faith[7] as a primary source of knowledge and wisdom toward

---

[5] Norbert Weiner, *Cybernetics: Or Control and Communication in the Animal and the Machine* (Paris, MIT Press, 1948). To this we can add more recent comments made by Michael Osborne, a professor in machine learning at the University of Oxford and co-founder of Mind Foundry. "Because we don't understand AI very well," he explains, "there is a prospect that it might play a role as a kind of new competing organism on the planet, a sort of invasive species that we've designed that might play some devastating role in our survival as a species." (*The Guardian*, May 30, 2023, "Risk of Extinction by AI should be global priority, say experts").

[6] Henry Kissinger, Eric Schmidt, and Daniel Huttenblocher, *The Age of AI* (Boston: Little, Brown and Company, 2022), 180, 226.

[7] Faith in this context is classically defined in Hebrews 11:1–40 (New International Bible): "Now faith is the assurance of things hoped for, the conviction of things not seen." In other words, faith is giving intellectual assent, for whatever reason, to a proposition that may not be susceptible to (scientific) proof. Medieval intellectual life was rooted in Judeo-Christian scripture, but also incorporated teachings of ancient Greece and Rome.

reason with its scientific toolbox and dazzling array of new technologies. It involved, in short, a deliberate mechanization of our concept of humanity and our institutions. With that came new values such as individualism, liberal democracy, moral relativism, and a new attitude to material success as the goal of human fulfilment, or progress.

Recently, thinkers and writers calling themselves "transhumanists" have taken this attitude a step farther with their argument that technological development constitutes an evolution of our species by other means—a further unfolding of the well-known Darwinian process of natural selection. They are particularly excited by the recent merging of biology and information technologies through direct brain-computer interfaces and implants designed to both repair brain damage and enhance "normal" brain functions. They also believe that a time will come in the reasonably near future when computers will have become more skilled at designing other intelligent computers than we are, at which stage machines will begin acting autonomously. The crossing of this threshold is what they call the "singularity."

This way of thinking about technology is fascinating from both philosophical and psychological points of view. Philosophically, the transhumanist project arises out of an Enlightenment, European humanist tradition of human liberation, and scientific discovery that emerged in the late seventeenth century. At the same time, though, it rejects—as manifestly ineffective—traditional humanist approaches to reaching its idealistic goals through education, self-control, charity, and other means, proposing technological solutions instead. There is a certain irony in this seen in the context of other technologies that have been designed by us to accommodate and advance our moral aspirations. Much more on that in what follows.

Paul Klee's angel of history gives us pause to wonder if the unintended consequences of technical progress—which is supposed to provide our salvation—will destroy us long before any sustainable stasis is reached. We must ask, what kind of "progress" leads to the destruction of humanity's basic habitat, even its basic identity?

This is a wrenching question because—I will be arguing—it goes to the root of our culture's long-standing faith in the sanctity of Enlightenment-era thought and its conceptions of progress. That may seem like a stretch, I realize. How could it be that more science and less superstition; more observation, less presumption; more reason, less emotion—all these good things—how could it be that they are what has led us into existential peril?

The short answer is that these ideas are not at fault. The problem lies in more fundamental attitudes to human nature itself that underlie the Enlightenment vision. A new and profoundly subversive worldview emerged in Enlightenment-era Europe in opposition to the Roman Catholic consciousness that held the commanding heights of the European intellectual landscape throughout the Middle Ages. The idea of an orderly universe ruled over by a benign, loving deity included a conception of the human being as having been made in "God's image," that is, participating in a fundamental, transcendent goodness.

According to the radical new Enlightenment perspective, however, humanity is effectively alone in the universe, left to its own devices by a Creator that seems to have retreated into distant, inactive retirement. Newly seen as products of a series of random, purposeless, natural processes, humans are condemned to coping as best we can with a grab bag of innate mental and physical traits generated through brutal evolutionary competition with one another, and with other species, in an uncaring world of scarcity and hazard. These "innate" characteristics were taken to be the constituents of "human nature" which, like other aspects of the natural world, was newly available to scientific understanding and manipulation via the mysterious gift of human reason and the revolutionary new tool we now refer to as the scientific method.

No longer was it possible to find comfort in the thought that we were made in God's image, that we had a place in a "great chain of being" that linked us to our maker, and that there was transcendent purpose to our existence. Instead, we were on track to a newly conceived destiny of constructing an earthly paradise, which would be based on the secure foundations of science and reason. In the early generations of the rationalist revolution (the Enlightenment era is often called the Age of Reason), there was high optimism, a near-euphoria, over human possibilities now that reason had been unchained from the fetters of intuition, moral judgment, and millennia of confining, conservative, religious, and mythological dogma.

Although—as was widely believed—we had evolved as slaves to our "passions," as innately selfish, greedy, aggressive, competitive, acquisitive creatures, these inherent and implacable human characteristics did not have to prove fatal to our prospects for earthly happiness.

Reason, that other defining trait of our species, would provide us with the social, legislative, and legal institutions by which we could mould our behaviour into a fair simulation of the altruism and charity so admired in the unenlightened, priest-ridden epoch Enlightenment thinkers dismissively styled the "Middle Ages." This era was so named because it linked the brilliant Classical eras of Greece and Rome to an even more brilliant and thoroughly modern Europe. This was the new grand narrative by which we were to live—by which our civilization was shaped—over the succeeding four hundred years.

And so, we arrive in our own confused times, the optimism of the Enlightenment rationalists with their modern worldview shattered by the accumulated wreckage of our failures. Our social, political, and economic institutions—inheritances of these philosophers and early scientific thinkers—have proved to be all too fallible. They fail to deliver on the promise of a morally justifiable level of comfort and happiness for all; a good life.

The desire to define a *good life* is a practice as old as philosophy itself. Paradoxically, in our era of late modernism, of advanced scientific knowledge and technological prowess, it is getting progressively more difficult to answer this undying question with conviction.

This is because "What is a good life?" is, unavoidably, a moral question—a question related to the nature and essence of good itself. "What is good?" may in fact be the most fundamental question anyone can ask. However, since the advent of modernity, mainstream Western thought has sought progressively to banish questions of morality and normative "value" from scientific and intellectual discourse. It has relegated this mode of questioning to the unscientific and therefore irrational realms of religious thought, "folk psychology," and metaphysical philosophy. We have all but lost the vocabulary necessary to engage the subject in our ordinary discourse.

If we are to learn to live together in the face of medical calamity and natural disaster, to reform the human environment in sustainable ways, to provide fundamental justice to the most vulnerable among us, we need to engage deeply in moral discourse. It will be important for all of us to be speaking the same language.

We will need to be fluent in the half-forgotten vocabulary of ethics and pay attention to the neglected processes of making moral judgements that will stand the test of time. We will need to understand the interconnectedness between science, the technology it produces, and the human values that we all agree are worth pursuing.

We will need to be able to define "progress" in a radically benevolent way.

2. What Science Can Teach

Few philosophers of any age have achieved the name recognition of Thomas Hobbes, the man who gave us the memorable description of human life in primeval times as "nasty, brutish, and short." He also coined the influential catchphrase, "reasoning is but reckoning," reducing thought to a sort of arithmetic in the fashion of his time. A prolific political theorist and proto-economist, Hobbes produced a body of political and economic ideas that have shown themselves to be extraordinarily tenacious despite their demonstrable shortcomings. His influence helped to shape the era of intellectual ferment that laid the foundations for modern science, capitalism, secularism, individualism, liberal democracy ... in a word, modernity. The era is variously referred to as the Age of Reason and the Enlightenment, and it coincided with a burst of discovery known as the Scientific Revolution.[8]

The son of a feckless Protestant pastor, Hobbes was born amid the terror and confusion of the aborted Spanish invasion of Elizabethan England in 1588. A well-to-do uncle staked him to a decent education culminating at Oxford, where he learned to hate conventional philosophy

8 The Enlightenment is traditionally, if somewhat arbitrarily, dated from 1650 to 1789. Closely related eras of overlapping intellectual ferment are dated as follows: the Scientific Revolution (1534–1687); the Protestant Reformation (1517–1685); and the Industrial Revolution (1760–1840). The Renaissance era, a time of rediscovery of many ancient Greek and Roman texts, is identified in relation to philosophers, theologians, and artists of the fourteenth to sixteenth centuries.

with its roots in Aristotle and its boundaries prescribed in Roman Catholic theology. He lived through the Protestant Reformation, which shook the foundations of medieval Christianity, and witnessed the unravelling of thousand-year-old social structures built up around the feudal system and the intellectual sovereignty of Roman Catholicism and its teaching orders. He would experience the blood-drenched English Civil Wars (1640–51); the execution of Charles I, Oliver Cromwell's brief republic and the restoration of the monarchy; an outbreak of bubonic plague that carried away a quarter of the population of London (1665–66); and the Great Fire that followed, destroying much of the central city over three days and nights.

As a bright young academic Hobbes became tutor to the scion of a rich and well-connected Cavendish family, and for much of his life he would owe his livelihood to their patronage. Through them he met such luminaries as Ben Jonson, the greatest playwright of the age after Shakespeare, as well as the philosopher and statesman Francis Bacon, an early and influential proponent of modern science and its processes.

As tutor to the Cavendish children and other aristocratic youths, Hobbes took several trips to Europe, and it was on one of those continental sojourns, in 1636, that he met with the great Galileo Galilei at the astronomer's picturesque Arcetri villa, just outside the walls of Florence.

Galileo was living out his waning years in indifferent health, drafting his great scientific opus on the laws of motion, under loose house arrest for having defied the Pope's injunction against promoting Copernicanism. This was the (by that time widely accepted) notion that the Sun, rather than the Earth, was at the centre of planetary motions, a theory Galileo had all but confirmed with his telescopic observations. But it was the astronomer's imperious insistence that science trumped all other sources of truth that landed him in hot water with Pope Urban VIII and led to the famous trial that has helped to define the debate between faith-based and scientific perspectives ever since.

Nothing has been recorded of their conversation behind the villa walls, but Galileo and Hobbes had in common an immoderate admiration for their own remarkable intellectual capacities. Furthermore, they both had a violent disdain for the science of Aristotle that had been the received wisdom in European universities throughout the Middle Ages. So, it may be imagined that their talk centered on the new mechanistic, materialistic view of nature that they, along with René Descartes, their contemporary and mutual acquaintance, were in the process of unleashing upon an unsuspecting world.

It was Descartes who proposed the celebrated tree analogy for the new outlook on philosophy, in which the roots are metaphysics, the trunk physics, and the branches the various disciplines including medicine, mechanics, and morals. Just as the tree is valued for its fruits, which we gather "not from the roots or the trunk but from the ends of the branches," Descartes wrote, it is the practical sciences that are most helpful in everyday life and most deserving of our attention. Rather than pursue Aristotle and the "speculative sciences" taught in the universities of his day, Descartes urged the development of "useful" sciences that he predicted would one day make us "masters and possessors of nature."[9]

What Galileo, Hobbes, and Descartes especially shared was a newfound confidence that it was within the grasp of human reason to know everything there is to know about the world and existence—to know, as Galileo put it, what God knows.

In retrospect, we see in this the birth of the scientific worldview, one of the most important intellectual landmarks in human history. Humankind, in the cold light of science no longer at the centre of the universe and no longer confident in the divinely ordained benevolence of nature, from now on had to take responsibility for its own destiny. And—it was believed by the scientific avant-garde with increasing confidence—humankind was perfectly capable of doing so.

Clerics, with their outdated appeals to divine providence as the chief source of human welfare, were advised stick to their knitting—theology and moral philosophy—and let science get on with unravelling the mysteries of the universe and putting that knowledge to work on behalf of progress in the struggle against nature. The defiant slogan gleaned from the revival of Plato and the Greek classics was "Man is the centre of all things" (Protagoras), and the iconic work of art was Leonardo da Vinci's "Vitruvian Man" (c. 1490), the male human figure, arms and legs outstretched, inscribed within a square and a circle indicative of the geometric universe.

According to the new worldview, only what was physically tangible and quantifiable had real existence. God, through most of recorded

---

9 René Descartes, *Discourse on Method* (1637).

history the object and the illumination of all philosophical enquiry, was for the rationalist thinkers—of whom Hobbes, Galileo, and Descartes were among the prototypes—merely a benign clockmaker, reduced to passively watching His invention run through its endless routines. Living creatures were nothing but complex machines that operated according to mechanical principles—the lone exception being humans, whom God had accessorized with a soul, the "ghost in the machine."[10] The once-universal notion that people had been made in the image of God, and were kin to the angels, would over time be replaced by mechanical metaphors that described humanity in terms of the latest and most advanced technologies, from the mechanical clock to the steam engine.

And with the excitement of new, scientific understanding came a growing existential anxiety. For the first time in history, philosopher-scientists were questioning the assumption that nature provided in ample measure everything humans needed for a comfortable life, and that the only problem for human society to resolve was the fair and equitable distribution of that God-given bounty. For these new thinkers, the workings of natural systems could no longer be taken for granted in their beneficial outcomes. No longer was it safe to assume, as Aristotle had, that there was purpose in nature's workings, and that that purpose was the achievement of Good—to assume that Good, in fact, was the engine that made the universe run.

For Aristotle, all natural motion, which included all growth and decay, was movement in the direction of Good, in the direction of the ultimate fulfilment of things. His views had deeply influenced Catholic scholastics throughout the Middle Ages. With early modernism, rationalist thinkers disengaged from such comfortable received wisdom.

Reason challenged not only cultural and religious dogma, but also one's superficial personal opinions. Reason was, as the philosopher Thomas Nagel says, "something each individual can find within himself, but at the same time has universal authority." Thus, "whoever appeals to reason purports to discover a source of authority within himself that is not merely personal, or societal, but universal—and that should also persuade others willing to listen to it."[11]

---

10 The phrase was coined by British philosopher Gilbert Ryle (1900–76) to mock Descartes's notion of mind and body as separate substances.

11 Thomas Nagel, *The Last Word* (New York: Oxford University Press, 1997), 5.

In the free-thinking climate that developed during the Protestant Reformation, the ability to reason was taken to be the defining feature of that new object of admiration: the self-sufficient human individual. Reason was also the sole, truly reliable, source of knowledge about the world. The mysterious power of the human mind to think logically and form sound judgements, especially when combined with the telescope, microscope, and other novel tools of observation, was taken to be a superior tool for decoding nature. It was seen as more trustworthy, certainly, than enigmatic religious texts or the surviving writings of classical civilization; more reliable even than direct sensory experience, which often misled and deceived.

The new freedom afforded by ideas of individualism and rationalism also implied new responsibility. For the first time, leading thinkers began to worry about previously unimaginable terrors such as overpopulation, the earliest references of which cropped up in Thomas More's *Utopia* (1516), in Francis Bacon's *Essays* (1597), and in Hobbes's own *Leviathan* (1651). Nature was coming to be seen in an entirely new way: not as God's bountiful gift to humanity, but as a potentially endangering environment that needed, urgently, to be understood and then conquered, as one might conquer and then administer an occupied people. Life was seen, increasingly, in terms of a struggle for existence in which science was an indispensable ally. At the same time, there was enormous confidence that nature *could* be managed, if only rational thought were liberated and given free rein.[12] Alexander Pope's famous epitaph to Newton, who was born in the year of Galileo's death, captures the optimistic aspect of the times in verse:

> Nature and nature's laws lay hid in night:
> God said, Let Newton be! and all was light.[13]

To which William Blake warily replied:

---

[12] For an exhaustive and thoroughly exhilarating treatment of this enormously important transition see Hans Blumenberg, *The Legitimacy of the Modern Age* (Cambridge: MIT Press, 1988), especially Chapter 5.

[13] "Letter to Thomas Butts," Nov. 22, 1802, in William Blake, *William Blake: The Complete Poems*, ed. Alicia Ostriker (New York: Penguin, 1977). Not to be outdone by Pope, Neil deGrasse Tyson, the astrophysicist and media personality, tweeted on Christmas morning 2017 that "On this day, long ago, a child was born who, by age 30, would transform the world. Happy Birthday Isaac Newton."

May God us keep
From single vision and Newton's sleep.

According to the rationalists, philosophy, understood broadly as the search for understanding of the world and humanity, ought henceforth to follow arithmetic and geometry in setting out its arguments and arriving at undeniable, self-evident truths or axioms. It should mimic as closely as possible the conventions and language of mathematics because ordinary, less precise language was subject to contamination by prejudices, superstitions, and theological dogma, all of which the new rationalist outlook was intent on pushing aside. So, as scientific thinking gained ground, more and more emphasis would be placed on *measurement*, on the processes and practices of attaching numerical values to what is observed as being fundamental to the attainment of reliable, objective knowledge.

Measurement, whether taken by weight scales, yardsticks, protractors, thermometers, barometers, sextants, or mechanical clocks, would be the means of decoding the language of nature, rendering it accessible to human comprehension. It could provide direct access to truth by eliminating subjective experience and its biases. A recorded, numerical measurement could be assumed to be the same for all observers.

Over time, quantity of data would come to be privileged over quality of insight, and notions of purpose in the workings of nature would be eclipsed by concrete numerical relationships, which proved to be superior in predicting outcomes and thus in exercising control over the natural environment. This shift in attention from purpose to prediction and control, from deductive top-down reasoning to bottom-up measurement and mathematical relationships, from philosophical to instrumental reason—from *why* to *how*—has justifiably been called the greatest revolution in human history. It would, however, lead ultimately to the present situation in which our access to information, and the power it confers, has gotten ahead of our ability to assess it from a perspective of moral responsibility.

Measurement and theory became closely entwined in science, in a process of abstraction from the concrete experience of nature to mathematical relationships. Something was lost in this process, as Raymond Tallis notes, and something else was gained:

> We may approach a body of liquid as something that has (say) depth, volume, weight, density, transparency, temperature, viscosity, temperature-dependent expansion and so on. We quantify those separately, though they cannot be separated in the material itself or as it is directly experienced. When we jump into a swimming pool, we cannot jump separately into its depth, its volume, its temperature, its viscosity, etc. ...The outcomes of measurement are located in a space increasingly remote from that occupied by the objects and events that are directly encountered. ... This is an important foundation for the most fundamental Copernican revolution: namely, one that displaces the subject from the centre of her world and relocates her as a small item in that world. ... Measurement starts the process that has taken us to a remarkable place from which we could look at our world from the outside.[14]

There is a seductive purity about what we know (or think we know) through measurement and instrumental reason, seemingly unaffected by the illusions of the senses, free of the errors of ancient authorities, or the delusions of religious revelation. It is a form of knowledge that appears to be direct, concrete, and unmediated, and which can be expressed with precision in axioms of apparently unquestionable truth. Who can doubt that 2+2 = 4 (and not 5), or that water at 100 degrees Celsius is hotter than water at 90 degrees Celsius?

And so, by the end of the seventeenth century, not just the Christian narrative of creation, but the science of Aristotle as well had been undermined by the rationalist writers Descartes, Galileo, Bacon, Hobbes, and the free-thinking Paris *philosophes*. In discovering numerical, mathematical relationships in nature, the early scientific explorers believed they were revealing a divine intelligence, in effect composing the texts for a "natural religion," or "natural philosophy," which would become simply "science."

The idea of a divinely ordained natural order accessible to reason and open to mathematical interpretation, and the notion that human nature derives from that basic structure, were taken up by Hobbes in his political thinking. The revolutionary ideas laid out in *De Cive* (1642) and *Leviathan* (1651) echo down the centuries to our own time, incorporated into current economic theory and other fields such as evolutionary biology and behavioural economics.

---

[14] Raymond Tallis, *Logos: The Mystery of How We Make Sense of the World* (Newcastle upon Tyne: Agenda Publishing, 2018), 23–4.

What little prosperity and security we enjoy, Hobbes said, we have *despite* who we are as humans. In our natural, pre-civilized state, ours was a dog-eat-dog world in which everyone was perpetually at war with everyone else, and life was unpleasantly precarious.

Our civilization and its satisfactions, he said, has its origins in fear, which drove primitive humans to voluntarily sacrifice their freedom and independence in exchange for the security and prosperity offered by an absolute ruler—his Leviathan—capable of imposing order.

It follows that it is the order imposed, often forcibly, by our political institutions and not any "better nature" or ethical insight that is responsible for our ability to become civilized and live together in harmony. In fact, Hobbes believed that good could only reasonably be defined as "that which is desired," and that rational individuals would naturally seek to maximize what is good for themselves.

Ethical decision-making, for Hobbes, is dependent on the situation at hand: where there is an absence of organized rule, we are free to do whatever it takes to maximize good for ourselves; where strong authority prevails (in the form of an absolute ruler, either a King or a despot) the chief moral obligation is to obey the ruler. This was shockingly at odds with both ordinary human intuition and Catholic teaching, and it led to Hobbes being vilified by many of his contemporaries. But he was in the grip of a big idea, of his ambition to develop a *theory of everything*, a grand, mechanistic model in which everything from the movements of the planets to the growth of trees to human emotions and the acquisition of knowledge could be described rationally, in terms of the same elementary materials and their prescribed, rule-based interactions. Though he had no real evidence to support it and had to ignore many contradicting factors, the idea of the human being as an innately competitive, self-interested creature responding mechanically to external pressures and influences fit his theory too well to be discarded.

Theory and theoretical models, in the sense of a set of rules or general principles that determine the operations of the thing explained, were certainly not new in Hobbes's day. The idea that the universe can be described in terms of geometry and mathematical ratios, for example, stretches all the way back to Pythagoras (580–500 BCE). Indeed, Pythagorean thinking can be seen to varying degrees in the works of many of the philosophers of Classical and Hellenistic Greece, notably

Plato and Aristotle, and in the great Greco-Roman astronomer Ptolemy (100–170 CE).

As Ptolemy expressed it, the point of Pythagorean, mathematics-based theorizing was to "save the appearances;" that is, to provide an explanation of natural phenomena that rendered them measurable, calculable, and predictable. It was understood by Ptolemy that such theoretical descriptions were not to be mistaken for the reality they modelled—theory's function was purely utilitarian. For example, the value of Ptolemy's system of planetary movements, in which the unmoving Earth is at the centre of the universe, lay in its ability to predict astronomical events such as eclipses and solstices and to aid in navigations at sea, all of which it did (and continues to do) admirably well. Whether it was *true* or not was, for Ptolemy, another kind of question altogether.

It is in the works of Hobbes's patron Francis Bacon (1561–1626), sometimes referred to as the father of modern science, that the status of theory is explicitly elevated to truth, according to the following formula: if a theory *saves* (i.e., provides an explanation for) *all the appearances* (i.e., observed phenomena), it *is* truth.

In other words, a coherent theoretical, mathematical depiction of nature and its workings is also a final explanation. In his *Novum Organum,* Bacon says, "there is a most intimate connection and almost an identity between the ways of human power and human knowledge ... That which is most useful in practice is most correct in theory." Reason, the ultimate authority, provides the connection.

Here, in its earliest formulations, modern science can be seen to be sliding into an intellectual rigidity amounting to dogmatism. In this intolerance lay the basis for Pope Urban VIII's epic dispute with Galileo and subsequent centuries of friction between religion and science. The issue was simple: while science, as Galileo and many of his contemporaries understood it, might be able to provide a complete understanding of the world, the Church insisted that it was only *one way* of knowing, and that the Judeo-Christian narrative, and moral knowledge in general, must be incorporated into any picture that claimed to be complete. Moral knowledge, metaphysical knowledge, although of a different nature than scientific knowledge, was nonetheless of equal, if not superior, validity.

Neither Galileo nor Bacon was irreligious (nor, for that matter was Hobbes), but Galileo bridled at having to accept the Church's monopoly on intellectual authority, particularly since its teachings incorporated so much of the science of Aristotle. The Church, for its part resisted, at times violently, the looming hegemony of reductionist, scientific thought—or as we now call it, modernism.

Bacon, a more conciliatory man than Galileo, argued that the Book of Nature (detailing God's works, and accessible to reason) and the Book of God (God's will, as revealed to prophets) were complementary and inseparable texts. At the core of his enthusiasm lay his belief that progress through science and technology was the means to achieve redemption for humankind and the imminent recovery of the perfection of Eden prior to the Fall.[15]

In Bacon's thought, reverence of a sort is found in full measure, but contemporary critics found these new ideas to be dangerously close to a narcissistic (and heretical) reverence for man rather than God. It was a view seen to be fatally tainted with pride, which, ironically, is the sin that led to the original expulsion of Adam and Eve from Eden. The tension between faith and science would play itself out in succeeding centuries as duelling heterodoxies: each was a heresy against the other. Philosophers today sometimes frame it as a "fact/value dichotomy."[16]

An aspect of Baconian science that helped to define it as essentially modern is its view of nature as an untamed and potentially dangerous environment that requires subjugation by force.[17] Ideas of individualism and of human exceptionalism vis-à-vis the natural world were implicit. Scientific experiments were "ordeals" in which an alienated nature was coerced by human adversaries into giving up her secrets. Bacon said, "we must put nature on the rack and compel her to bear witness."

This objectifying, combative approach to nature was a fundamental departure from the Classical Greek and medieval Christian notions of nature as Providence, as the divinely-provided, protective, and nurturing home depicted in the story of Eden. It also reflects an aspect of Enlightenment-era individualism and humanism that was strongly anthropocentric, that put humanity in a sense outside of nature at the

---

15 And Descartes, believing that science made humanity the "maîtres et possesseurs de la nature" [masters and possessors of nature] nevertheless relied on the existence of God, a supremely perfect being, as foundational to his entire philosophic edifice.

16 Hilary Putnam, *The Collapse of the Fact/Value Dichotomy and Other Essays* (Cambridge: Harvard University Press, 2002).

17 See, Thomas Moore's *Utopia* (1516) for a similar perspective.

moral centre of the world, a perspective that has been revealed in our own time to be highly problematic. More on that later.

The linkage between science and survival proposed by Bacon and his contemporaries has had a continuing influence on the so-called hard, or physical, sciences and their research aims, and on the human sciences as well. Science as a continuing, expensive enterprise came to be treated as an insurance policy—costly, but something we can't afford to be without given the endangering character of nature. "We cannot live without science," writes historian Hans Blumenberg, "[but] that is itself largely an effect produced by science. It has made itself indispensable."[18]

In today's terms, to in any way restrain scientific enquiry or technological research and development is thus to increase, or at least fail to minimize, existential risk. Open-ended scientific curiosity must be actively encouraged, not simply for its own sake, but because it is simply prudent to do so.[19] Those limits we impose on research and experimentation are, for the most part, promulgated and administered by scientists themselves; the "bioethicist" is an example of a new specialty concerned primarily with broad implications of both the processes and societal impact of research, in this case in biology. The many branches of science, we are told, need their own ethical frameworks, each informed by the demands of research. The risks of conflict of interest within this arrangement are obvious.

It is not just scientific practice that can be interrogated from a moral perspective. The idea of scientific curiosity bears examination as well. If scientific practice and the limitations it self-imposes are open to question, what about the assumption that all scientific curiosity is laudable?

Curiosity in a general sense has of course always been with us, in the form of a preference for knowledge over uncertainty and risk. During the Middle Ages, faith in a benevolent and protective God led to a kind of fatalism, a view that it was improper and even irreligious to enquire too deeply into mysteries of the natural order. And in even earlier times, Classical Greek philosophers thought the purpose of curiosity and scientific theory was not to make life possible, but to make it happy.

18 Blumenberg, *Legitimacy of the Modern Age*, 231.

19 Note that market capitalism's globalized competitive ethos, with its emphasis on the existential need for continuous economic growth, reinforces this historic bias. See Chapter 6 of Blumberg's *The Legitimacy of the Modern Age*.

Since modernity and the Scientific Revolution of the sixteenth and seventeenth centuries, however, we have been encouraged to believe that scientific curiosity is not just necessary to survival in a hostile environment, but is a virtue in its own right, essential to moral progress and therefore worthy of protection and encouragement.

But even a casual knowledge of the history of science and technology justifies the suspicion that not all scientific curiosity is virtuous or morally acceptable. Sometimes it may be immoral and in need of restraint. The difficulty is in seeing which cases are which. Take, for example, germ-line genetic manipulation, making changes in the DNA of plants, animals, and even humans—alterations that will be inherited by subsequent generations and are therefore ineradicable once released into the gene pool.

In early 2023, the US Food and Drug Administration approved clinical trials of new human brain implant technology that would provide direct, two-way computer-to-brain communication. The initial targets of the Elon Musk-owned "Neuralink" project are complex neurological disorders that don't respond well to conventional medicine. But Musk and others in the field have often speculated about using the technology to enhance human cognition, sensory perception, and athletic abilities. A common lay criticism is that such experiments are "playing God;" that they are above and beyond legitimate human curiosity, mainly because there is no way to predict all foreseeable outcomes. But this is a position based largely on instinct, and difficult to sustain outside the context of religion. Who is to say what's out of bounds? Who says scientists shouldn't play God if the stakes are high enough? Who says scientists aren't in fact doing God's work?

Here is where the modern ethical "specialist" steps in. From the perspective of a bioethicist, proper and legitimate scientific restraint on the curiosity of bioengineers, for example, might be justified by evidence that their work involves a reckless or poorly informed tampering with nature that could result in harmful, unanticipated, and possibly irreversible consequences for our species.

Framed this way, the issue can be reduced to risk management, another modern specialty. The question from this perspective is not, "Ought we to tamper?" but rather, "How much tampering (or 'enhancement') is justified, given the predicted level of risk and the projected benefits?" And too often the assessment is made in pursuit of a post-hoc rationalization for work already underway or completed.

But risk-management calculations would seem inadequate for the task assigned to them when—as in so much of current scientific and technical endeavour—the stakes are literally incalculable. For one thing, any admission of risk will typically be weighed against promised benefits that are frequently framed as biblical in import. Nothing less is promised by genetic researchers and engineers than the elimination of disease and, more recently, the radical extension of human lifespan—in effect, the return of humanity to its original state of Edenic perfection. On the other side of the equation, any listing of risks will, by definition, be incomplete—the essence of risk is, after all, the unknown and unexpected.

Thus, in many risk-management exercises the question comes to be posed this way: what current risk can possibly outweigh incalculable benefits such as these—benefits that are being promised not just to us, but to all future generations? Any utilitarian calculation of "the greatest good for the greatest number" will almost certainly support those whose cry is "Full speed ahead!" Yet, tampering with the human genetic heritage seems somehow inherently wrong to many, especially when it is realized that the most passionate proponents of these technologies are, as we will see,[20] speaking for corporations that stand to profit from patented techniques, and are ill-equipped to consider moral issues.

Biologist Sarah Sexton captured the issue perfectly with the wry title of an essay on human genetic engineering written following the birth of the cloned sheep, Dolly, at the Roslin Institute in Scotland in 1996.[21] "If cloning is the answer," she wrote, "what was the question?"[22]

What, indeed, is the question? It might be something like, "How can we assist nature in perfecting the human species?" But that won't do, because science does not recognize any *telos* or destination in the processes of evolution—there is no "goal," (let alone "good" or "bad" goals) so

20 See Chapter 7.

21 Dolly was born July 5th, 1996, but her birth was not publicly announced until February 23rd, 1997 in the British newspaper, *The Observer*, and the scientific journal, *Nature*, because the Roslin Institute wanted to obtain a patent on the nuclear cloning technique. The patent covers all mammals, including humans.

22 Sarah Sexton, "If Cloning is the Answer, What Was the Question? Power and Decision-Making in the Geneticization of Health," *International Journal of Sustainable Development* 4, (2001): 407–33.

what could "improvement" mean? To suggest that genetic interventions are merely assisting in a natural evolutionary process is to believe that Darwinian evolution is itself directed toward "perfecting" species, which is not the case. Evolutionary change tends to settle out when a "good enough" level of development is achieved.[23] The idea of perfection in this context is incoherent. Perfection is a value-laden term, and therefore, by their own definition, out of bounds to scientists.[24]

This leaves us no choice but to deal with the difficult word, "perfect," as both verb and adjective. If we are to offer a credible justification for this kind of research, we are compelled to try to understand what a more perfect human being—indeed, a more perfect human race—might be. This is quite obviously a philosophical as much as a scientific question, and so we are obliged to elevate the discussion to the realm of moral enquiry.

In what *moral* sense, then, might germ-line genetic engineering be considered "above and beyond" legitimate human curiosity? Clearly, the questions we need to ask concern humanity and its goals and purposes, as opposed to technical questions about risk and benefit. Where do we draw the line between the elimination of genetic defect or disease and tweaking "desirable" traits like high IQ or athletic ability? Without moral knowledge of this kind, how can we even know what a "benefit" might be?

Not just morality, but reason itself tells us that science and the technical innovations it supports cannot be carried on responsibly without parallel research into their moral implications. That research involves, inevitably, tackling at some level the oldest question in moral philosophy: *What is good?*

---

23 Daniel S. Milo, *Good Enough: The Tolerance for Mediocrity in Nature and Society* (Cambridge: Harvard University Press, 2019).

24 Gene-editing in human embryos using CRISPR technology is a slightly different issue, in that it is focused more directly on disease eradication. While this may sound morally justifiable, the risks involved in germ-line DNA editing are not less daunting than in cloning. See, for example: Nicholas Gutierrez, "What's Next for the Gene-Edited Children from the CRISPR Trial in China?" *New Scientist*, June 29, 2022.

3. What Morality Can Teach

Can universally valid moral principles be established by human reason alone? For Enlightenment-era scientific theorists, it seemed an urgent issue. "What we have to realize," writes historian Carl Becker, "is that in those years God was on trial. Enlightenment-era readers and writers of books alike wanted to know,

> ... were they living in a world ruled by a beneficent mind, or in a world ruled by an indifferent force? ... And we can no more think of a Philosopher ignorant of, or indifferent to, this question than we can think of a modern philosopher ignorant of, or indifferent to, quantum theory."[25]

There was an uneasiness in the radical rationalist movement of the eighteenth century about demolishing the architecture of Christian morality without providing a replacement. The French encyclopedist Denis Diderot (1713–84), referring to theologians, said, "it is not enough to know more than they do; it is necessary to show them that we know more than they do; it is necessary to show that we are better, and that philosophy makes more good men than sufficient or efficacious grace." Any philosopher who would demolish the Christian foundations

[25] Carl L. Becker, *The Heavenly City of the 18th-Century Philosophers* (London: Yale University Press, 1932), 73–4.

of morality without supplying a natural substitute would be seen, with justification, as "an apologist for wickedness."[26]

This dilemma would lead, in time, to the divorce of philosophy and science: where there had for the previous two millennia been a single knowledge-seeking vocation called philosophy, there would now be two separate pursuits—natural philosophy, or science, and moral philosophy, essentially a catch-all category for pressing questions science was unequipped or unwilling to tackle.

Science would limit its curiosity exclusively to "well-posed problems;" questions that can be defined clearly and precisely enough to guarantee that a "scientific" answer can be found. All else was to be pared away. In practice, this would lead to all references to the metaphysical, to a divine or transcendent order, being expunged from science. The only legitimate questions could be framed by "what" and "how." The question "why" would be largely out of bounds and consigned to philosophy since it did not produce useful knowledge—in particular, knowledge that can be turned over to technologists for toolmaking.

However, the issue of overarching goals, of some transcendent destination or purpose at work in the world, refused to go away. It was too closely attached to the innate human sense of morality to be easily abandoned. And so, as a substitute for the providential goals or *telos* prescribed for humanity in the medieval Christian narrative of a loving and caring God, modern science substituted two important, quantifiable concepts: *posterity* and *progress*. The goal of scientific endeavour was to bless posterity with the results of scientific advances in the form of improved health, longevity, material abundance, and security from the ravages of nature; that is, to leave a better world to future generations through progress.

But moral issues cannot be evaded so easily. To pursue the question of what is meant by "better" in any human context is to arrive inevitably in the deep woods of morality, facing the ultimate question—what is good? Here in the forest, where paths are often indistinct and poorly marked, a compass is an asset.

Most of us do our best to minimize the intrusion of deep moral deliberations into our public and professional lives, secure in the belief that issues of moral value are for most purposes already well-defined by the system, by the social, legal, and institutional rules of liberal democratic

26 Ibid, 82.

society with which we grow up and follow throughout our lives.[27] Or perhaps we are among those who continue to subscribe to the moral mandates of a major religion, an ethical monotheism such as Judaism, Christianity, or Islam. In either case, if we were to weigh the moral import of every action we perform, we'd go insane, or at least be rendered totally unproductive.

When we do think about morality in any depth, our default position is to take the existence of good for granted. Good seems real, rather than imaginary. The concept is basic to our vocabularies, in every language; we define wickedness and evil in terms of its absence. We feel we know normative good when we see it, in every field of existence and experience. This confidence is remarkable, because it persists in the face of the overwhelmingly skeptical "official" position presented to us in our secular institutions, including our schools, universities, and corporate work environments. But, despite that confidence, if we are asked to *define* good, most of us are stumped.

We all know what a good deal is, what a good dog is, what a good holiday is. We speak fluently of good friends and neighbours, good children, and women, and men. Even "good" wars. But what do we mean? Good clearly has emotive meaning to us—its presence makes us feel warm and fuzzy, or righteous and self-assured. But the cognitive meaning, the meaning grasped by thought processes, is more difficult to pin down. To be defined as cognitively good must stand for an objective property, so that to call something "good" is not merely to express a preference or a feeling but to make a true or false statement. A statement about the presence of some*thing*. What, then, is good itself?

Early modern eighteenth and nineteenth-century scientific attitudes, as well as an influential stream of early twentieth-century philosophy called logical positivism, all support the view that this is a futile question; that it is not just "poorly-posed," but meaningless nonsense. It would take us too far afield to pursue logical positivism and its primary proponents (Rudolf Carnap, Carl Hempel, Ludwig Wittgenstein, and others in the 1920s Vienna Circle) but its influence on both academic and popular thinking about truth and meaning was, and remains,

---

[27] My use of the terms "ethics" and "morality" herein follow the widely accepted distinction in moral realism: *morality* deals with the common-sense assessments and behaviours of everyday living and *ethics* with the theoretical constructs that shape and provide rational nuance to morality.

substantial. Essentially, we are asked to believe that the only "realities" worth thinking about are material in nature, and that science, rooted in logic and mathematics, has exclusive access to knowledge. Thus, science is the sole arbiter of what is real and true, and all else is literal *non-sense.*

This radical viewpoint, a twentieth-century throwback to eighteenth-century rationalism, is no longer as fashionable as it once was among philosophers, or even scientists. Quantum physics, though supreme among contemporary cutting-edge "hard" sciences, cannot avoid the recognition that its many paradoxes may ultimately be unresolvable within the conventional boundaries of science. Nils Bohr, a respected founder of the field, has said that the essential lesson of quantum physics is that we are a part of the nature we seek to understand, and the techniques we employ in investigating it must be seen to be interactions among component parts of the phenomena being examined. The detached "outside observer" does not exist. And if that is the case, as we try to understand the world through science we must recognize the fact that our knowledge-making practices are interactive processes in which both the observer and the observed are affected by their mutual engagement or entanglement. Under such conditions, truly "objective" knowledge is unattainable.

So perhaps it would be wise, based on prudence alone, to trust our instincts that good exists, and consider all the possibilities. As the poet Alice Fulton said, believing in something and having faith in our instincts can sometimes lead us to otherwise undiscoverable truth. Sometimes,

> We have to meet the universe halfway.
> Nothing will unfold for us unless we move toward what
> Looks to us like nothing: faith is a cascade.[28]

Aristotle put it this way:

> If, then, there is some end of the things we do, which we desire for its own sake (everything else being desired for the sake of this), and if we do not choose everything for the sake of something else (for at that rate the process would go on to infinity, so that our desire would be empty and vain), clearly this must be the good and the chief good. Will not the knowledge of

[28] Alice Fulton, "Cascade Experiment," in *Powers of Congress* (Louisville: Sarabande Books, 1989).

> it, then, have a great influence on life? Shall we not, like archers who have a mark to aim at, be more likely to hit upon what is right? If so, we must try, in outline at least, to determine what it is, and of which of the sciences or capacities it is the object.[29]

In addressing the problem of normative values many Western philosophers, drawing on Plato, have described good (or sometimes, *the* good, or good *itself*) as existing in a metaphysical realm beyond ordinary material reality, as a genuine, though intangible, dimension of existence. Here's the general idea: in Plato's formula, everything in the concrete and material world as we know it is merely an imperfect approximation of its *ideal form*, the perfect entity that lives in a higher realm of being where good itself exists. A similar idea was taken up nearly two thousand years later in the early Enlightenment philosophy of Baruch Spinoza (1632–77), for whom the material world—nature—is synonymous with God, and vice-versa. Thinking, reasoning, people are able, with effort, to seek out the tools and information they need to bring them closer to the knowledge of good, and in so doing they are creating happiness for themselves. They are instinctively "led to seek for means which will bring [them] to this pitch of perfection [i.e., happiness], and call everything which will serve as such means a true good."[30] In other words, good, for humans, is to be found in the acquisition of knowledge that leads to happiness by bringing them closer to the ultimate good that is God and nature.

Descriptions like these are evocative, beautiful, even compelling, but they are not very serviceable in our increasingly hectic and distracted contemporary world. The result has been that the quandary over the nature of goodness has been neglected in modern moral philosophy which, like everything else in the modern world, has tended to tilt toward the practical and instrumental.

To address this problem and re-incorporate the good into everyday ethical discourse, a growing number of today's moral thinkers have taken a position that does not deny the validity of metaphysical knowledge as a hypothesis, but instead tries to align it with current science. What they propose is a compromise between the cosmologies that place good outside

29 Aristotle, *Nicomachean Ethics* 1:2 (c. 325 BCE). in W. D. Ross (trans,), *Aristotle* (New York, Meridian Books, 1959).

30 Spinoza, *Ethics* (1677), trans. G. H. R. Parkinson (New York: Random House, Everyman Classics, 1989), 2 iii.

the world of *things*, and a more modern materialist view, which is more amenable to the modern scientific mind. On this view good, rather than (or perhaps in addition to) existing "beyond being," is actually *real*—ineffable, perhaps, but as much a part of everyday existence as gravity. Like gravity, good exists in the world and influences events in ways that are readily observable, even though, like gravity, its precise nature remains a mystery. According to this view, good would exist even if we didn't—or as philosophers say, good is mind-independent. It is real.

While it is the case that the existence of good is not demonstrable in scientific terms—it can't be weighed or measured or recorded by instruments—it is nonetheless *knowable* in the cognitive, and not merely emotive, feel-good sense of the word. We can intuit its presence and authority through our innate moral sensibility. We can then confirm our intuition by careful observation of our own behaviour, and that of others, over time and across cultures, and by employing the processes of sound reasoning to draw a reliable conclusion from all this data.

The most formidable resistance to rationalism and thus to modernist philosophy in general was provided by the German philosopher Immanuel Kant (1724–1804). The depth of his influence is reflected in the fact that European philosophy is today often divided into pre- and post-Kantian perspectives. No other thinker has cast a more penetrating light on modern perceptions of good. Importantly, he brought rational thought, together with knowledge gleaned from empirical observation or sensory input, into a moral philosophy that illuminates ancient moral wisdom and lays out a rigorously modern, reason-based approach to ethics.[31]

In his general theory of knowledge, Kant was wary of placing too much faith in the powers of reason to provide a complete picture of the world, favouring instead a greater reliance on the data from empirical observation. But when he turned to ethics, he took a different position, arguing that empirical information carries no moral content, or—as William James put it, things on their own "have no moral character at all."

---

[31] In some ways it is the modern equivalent of the achievement of Saint Thomas Aquinas (1225–1274) in reconciling Aristotle's empirical science with the tradition of Christian knowledge-seeking as exemplified in the University of Paris and other great medieval institutions of learning run by the church. Aquinas's influence is credited with allowing modern science to flourish alongside, rather than in opposition to, medieval Christian scholarship.

Moral thought, Kant said, is rooted instead in a universal, rational principle of rightness or goodness, which is as self-evident and undeniable as the principles of logic, and which, for all practical purposes, can be relied upon with absolute certainty.

His argument unfolds like this: it is an empirical fact that humans have wants and desires, which they seek to satisfy through action. These impulses are neither moral nor immoral on their own; they simply exist. But there is a rational principle, a framework, a form of moral law, that can tell us whether our actions taken with respect to these impulses are either right or wrong, moral or immoral.

Like human reason itself, Kant's moral law has two essential characteristics: universality and necessity. To be human is, by definition, to be a rational being. Moral law, an expression of human reason, is universal in that it applies to *all* human conduct, and it *necessarily* does this. No behaviour falls outside the frame.

Moral law is given a practical everyday application when Kant highlights the fact that humans are both rational and *social* creatures. We understand and can empathize with others of our species. In this context, one's moral behaviour, if it is to obey the law that is both universal and necessary, can only be conduct that we would wish to be followed by everybody else.

In other words, to act morally in any given situation is to behave in a way that you would want to be mandatory for all other people in the same situation. If you can't in good conscience make that wish, then your action is wrong. No exceptions, no special treatment for oneself. Or as Kant puts it in his famous dictum: "Act only on that maxim whereby thou canst at the same time will that it should he a universal law."

This is the Golden Rule of old, dressed in abstract, philosophical garb. Kant, of course, recognized this, but he would have argued that such thinking has always been the product of human rationality, even before reason had become a topic of human curiosity and enquiry. The prophets who promulgated the edict to "love thy neighbour as thyself" were expressing rational moral law, however much they may have believed they were relaying instructions from on high. (Or perhaps, Kant might have conceded, both were true.)

Kant proposes that his reason-based morality can be tested and confirmed empirically, in everyday life. We can observe the moral judgements we make about our own and others' behaviour, and then try to work out why we react in the way we do: what principles are behind our judgements? Disappointed by the breaking of a promise, we might ask why it was the wrong thing to do, and whether it is always wrong to break promises. Can we make exceptions for ourselves, for our own convenience and gain?

We will be forced to conclude, Kant says, that a world in which such exceptions were permissible, in which anyone could break any promise anytime, would be an intolerable place to live. Again, a moral law must both necessary and universal: it is a "categorical imperative" in Kantian terminology and must be obeyed without exception. It is not a means to an end, like a government policy statement or a corporate ethical guideline, but an end in itself. Another well-known example of the categorical imperative is that humans should never be used as means to ends; only as ends in themselves.

The personal implications of all of this for you and me are well-described by E. A. Burtt:

> So far as our individual conduct is concerned, this amounts to subordinating the natural desire for personal happiness to the demands of social duty. So far as our relations with others are concerned, it means avoidance of all temptation to exploit them as instruments to the furtherance of our own purposes; it means treating them with the ultimate respect which we wish to be treated ourselves. This moral end is necessary because it derives from the nature of reason, which is the supreme and distinctive essence of man.[32]

Kant explains the connection between intuition and reason in ethical thought by drawing an analogy between our *senses* and our *desires*. Our senses connect us to the outside world; our desires make us aware of our internal needs and wants. In the first case, we can apply reason to the sensory inputs to help understand what our senses are telling us, to know what actions to take in interacting with the physical world. In the case of moral or ethical experience we apply reason to the data provided by our desires to help us decide the right course of action. As biological beings, our desires cause us to act in such a way that will lead to their satisfaction or fulfilment, the goal being personal happiness or well-being.

The catch is that *reason* tells us that the selfish pursuit of personal, sensual satisfaction is the very definition of immorality. Why is this the case? Why

---

[32] E. A. Burtt, *Types of Religious Philosophy, Revised Edition* (New York: Harper and Bros., 1939).

is it that, in reason, selfishness amounts to immorality? Kant explains that reason, when applied to moral conduct rather than to scientific understanding, must satisfy two characteristics: its conclusions, to be valid, must be both universal and necessary. Therefore, what reason brings to morality is the idea of the *rule of law*, the familiar notion that certain laws must be obeyed (necessity) and obeyed by everyone (universality). Reason tells us that this is a requirement for the flourishing of human life. Chaos reigns without the rule of moral law, and unhappiness reigns with it.

For Kant, moral knowledge is different from empirical, scientific knowledge in that it is definitive and unchanging. Although good exists independently of sensory experience, we can know it because we are, uniquely, rational creatures and as such we are in touch with the essence of the universe.

Another approach to proving the existence of a hypothetical phenomenon or entity like Good is through a process called proof by necessity. This is the idea that if a concrete reality—an established scientific fact—can only be explained in terms of the existence of something else, *then that other thing must exist* even though it may have yet to be discovered. The evidence for its existence is the fact that it explains a known, confirmed reality that would otherwise be inexplicable.

A recent, instructive example concerns the discovery of the Higgs boson particle, whose existence was finally confirmed in 2012 at the CERN laboratories in Switzerland after a search that lasted almost half a century. The existence of the particle was proposed by quantum physicists in the early 1960s. They sought to confirm the basic cosmology called the Standard Model of quantum physics which holds that everything in the universe is made from a few fundamental particles whose relationships are governed by four fundamental forces. These are gravity, electromagnetism, and the so-called "strong" and "weak" forces found at the atomic level.

Confirmed by many experiments, and by mathematical equations of remarkable symmetry, the Standard Model nevertheless had a suppurating flaw, one that threatened its very foundations. The equations that describe the theory show that all the force-*delivery* particles, or bosons, associated with these four fundamental force fields (one could also say "comprising" these fields) should have zero mass. Unfortunately, some bosons had been shown experimentally to have a lot of mass. If the equations, and the Standard Model, were to be preserved, some explanation would have to be found for the phenomenon of massive bosons. In 1964, one was proposed in the form of an as-yet-undiscovered, in principle unobservable, fifth fundamental field that pervades the universe and is responsible for mass in particles.

This is the "Higgs field," named for one of the theorists behind the idea, Peter Higgs of the University of Edinburgh. The longer particles interacted with the field, the theory went, the more massive they'd become. Some particles interacted with it a lot and were massive; others, like quarks, only a little; and still others, like photons, not at all and they have zero mass as a result. If the Higgs field existed, it would have to have some force-delivery particles or bosons associated with it. So, the search began for a new, high-mass, fundamental particle scientists now call the Higgs boson.

Nearly fifty years later, in 2012, strong evidence for such a particle was observed by atom-smashing scientists operating the large hadron collider at CERN. Today it is believed that all sub-atomic particles that have mass derive it from interactions with the Higgs field. The Higgs field, however—by consensus a fundamental, or perhaps *the* fundamental feature of our universe—*cannot itself be observed*.

As with other force fields, all we can know about it must be learned from its effect on subatomic particles, which we *can* observe, for example by photographing the trails they leave in so-called bubble chambers associated with particle accelerators like the one at CERN. In the case of the Higgs field, however, even that bit of visual confirmation is denied researchers: the Higgs boson can't be detected in a bubble chamber like other particles.

I explore this breakthrough in modern physics and cosmology in some detail to make a point about one way in which knowledge is constructed, not just in science, but in moral philosophy as well. The analogy with the existence of good in the universe seems obvious. Good is a phenomenon whose existence is necessary to explain everyday realities of the world—properties we call justice, beauty, dignity, and love in all its manifestations—all of which have direct, observable, and even quantifiable effects on the behaviour of humans and other sentient beings. All these properties are on exhibit in the global laboratory billions of times every minute of every day. As was the case with the Higgs field, the proof of the existence of good lies in the demonstrable existence of those *otherwise unexplainable* phenomena.

Soon after the announcement of the Higgs boson discovery, to the chagrin of many scientists, it acquired the name "the God particle." This was due to its association with the ubiquitous, omnipresent, all-creating Higgs field and the field's resemblance to Spinoza's perfect God-in-nature.[33]

Whether or not the popularity of the phrase can be attributed to an irrational religious impulse in humanity that is responsible for thousands of years of theology, as many claim, it still raises a question. It's worth asking: is it any less probable to ascribe the basis of a thing's existence to an intentional God than to a fortuitous, hypothetical phenomenon—an immaterial force-field whose essence is known to us only through experimental evidence obtained through some of the most complex technologies ever developed? Whose evidence described and communicated in terms of mathematics is so abstract and complex that, in all the world, only a handful of specially trained individuals can comprehend it? Which, one might ask, is the more probable explanation for the cosmic trajectory of the cosmos from the Big Bang to life, and consciousness, and to value? Or are these two explanations, as Spinoza might argue, saying the same thing? We will look further into this.

Yet another, satisfyingly concrete approach to the moral realist's challenge of defining good is taken by the American pragmatist philosopher William James (1842–1910). He asks us to imagine a purely material world in which sentient life and consciousness do not exist—say, Earth, 3.8 billion years ago, before the evolution of bacteria. In such a world, good cannot exist, for how can one thing, one purely physical fact, be *better* than another? As James says, "betterness is not a physical relation. In its mere material capacity, a thing can no more be good or bad than it can be pleasant or painful."[34] Good reaches beyond the material fact, to relationships with the other: good *at* something, good *for* something, better *than* some other thing.

Now, introduce a single sentient being to our imaginary world, and the possibility arises for good (and bad) really to exist. Moral relations now have their *status* in that being's consciousness. Insofar as she feels anything to be good, she *makes* it good. It is *good for her*; and being good, for her, is absolutely good, for she is the sole creator of values in that

33 The coinage is credited to Nobel laureate Leon Lederman and his 1993 book *The God Particle*.

34 William James, "The Moral Philosopher and the Moral Life," in *Pragmatism and Other Essays* (New York: Washington Square Press, 1972).

universe, and outside of her opinion things have no moral character at all. James's point is that good must be *realized* in order to exist, in order to be real. And it can only be realized in the mind of a sentient being, which *feels* one thing to be right, another to be wrong.

Now add a second sentient being to this world, and it too will have its own feelings and ideas about what is good and bad, right and wrong. And then add a third and a fourth, and so on. We can assume that with the growth of sentient populations, ideas of good can broaden from "what's good for me," or "what feels good" to considerations of whether goods of others might, on consideration, turn out to be "good for me" as well. This is the beginning of ethical thinking, and it moves from there to an ethic of genuine charity, or selfless giving. In the end, James says, if good is identified with the satisfaction of demands or desires of individual sentient beings, then good in the sense of *the* good, can be assumed to be found in the collective satisfaction of as many individual desires, or demands, as possible.

Of course, not all demands can be satisfied at the same time, because there will be conflicts and contradictions. In the ironing-out of these issues, we are engaged in ethical thinking, and the prospect is that as time passes, conflicts will diminish (though never disappear). It is by any measure a powerful knowledge-generating process, and it bends toward the good, as best as we can define the concept. It could scarcely do otherwise, given that it is driven by individual judgements as to what is good, in the broadest sense, for each person (i.e., what satisfies their personal desires).

These desires will evolve and broaden over time, with experience, knowledge, and changing circumstances. As James said, "everywhere the ethical philosopher must wait on fact … and the *highest* ethical life … consists at all times in breaking the rules which have grown too narrow for the actual case." There is, he says, "but one unconditional commandment, which is that we should seek incessantly, with fear and trembling, so to vote and to act as to bring about the very largest total universe of good which we can see."[35]

As is the case in science, we can assume that as ethical thought proceeds, with growing populations of sentient beings working in cooperation, certain foundational relations or laws will emerge to organize what would otherwise be a hopelessly chaotic field. Some kinds of demands will be seen in retrospect to have been harmful and bad, while others may turn out to have real merit, and these will be remembered and reinforced. If,

[35] Ibid, 231. We can assume that the similarity to Kant's thought here is not entirely fortuitous.

as some have suggested, Neolithic cave paintings of animals and human-animal interactions are ethical in content—that is, having to do with human relationships with the animals they must kill to sustain life—then it's safe to say that the ruminations from which those guiding principles can gradually emerge have been going on for at least twenty thousand years, as populations of homo sapiens grew from a few tens of thousands to today's multiple billions.[36]

As sensible and down-to-earth as James's argument may seem, it remains hanging in mid-air. It does not clearly define the good we are enjoined to "seek incessantly, with fear and trembling." He recognizes this and wonders, in concluding his essay: what if that first sentient being, the initial bringer of values to an otherwise material world, is a Creator of infinite knowledge—i.e., God? That would surely simplify moral deliberations, because divine values would presumably form a comprehensive moral code of unchallengeable authority. But it would also make the consideration of good a metaphysical project. One for philosophers and metaphysicians rather than physicists.

In the end, it makes little difference whether our intuition leads us to accept the existence of good as a reality, or if we are led to that conclusion by chains of reasoning provided by philosophers, or by revelations of religious teachers. The acceptance of the reality of good makes consideration of its place in the world impossible to avoid in *any* coherent description of existence, including science. It suggests that, in this world in which good is as much an everyday reality as gravity—that is, in the world as we experience it as human beings—meaning and purpose are possible, even inescapable. The existence of good makes it so; it reveals an irresistible horizon, a goal; one that creates an obligation.

In contemporary philosophy, this naturalistic approach to moral thought is called "critical moral realism."[37] It proposes that good is a fundamental, though ultimately indescribable, element of our reality, a mind-independent feature of the universe. The adjective "critical" is important. It is intended to signify that the affirmation of the reality of good is something more than just

---

36 Karen Armstrong, *The Case for God* (New York: Knopf, 2009).

37 Some of the better-known adherents and proponents include Hannah Arendt, Theodor Adorno, Erich Fromm, Herbert Marcuse, Walter Benjamin, Jurgen Habermas, Bernard Lonergan, Terry Eagleton, Mary Midgley, Hilary Putnam, Zygmunt Bauman, Ian Barbour, and Michael Polanyi.

a theoretical proposition, and that it is possible to test or critique its validity in much the same way as we might test a scientific hypothesis.[38]

There are, in other words, such things as *moral facts*, which rely for their authority on knowledge of and direct experience with good, and which can be verified through a process directly analogous to the one used in science, where provisional facts (or hypotheses) are tested by a formal process of replicating observations and experiments. In practice, this shared process amounts to an unending attempt to either confirm (always provisionally) or falsify (often definitively) established knowledge. It is a process that has led us, in physics, astronomy, and cosmology, from one revolution to the another. It has led us from Ptolemy, to Copernicus, to Galileo, to Newton, to Einstein, to the quantum mechanics of the early twentieth century, and beyond into territory where today's hard-nosed physicists are unnerved by mathematical models that point to an underlying, spooky reality called the Higgs field.

In science, and in moral thought, those facts which first seem to accurately describe reality, and then successfully resist repeated attempts at falsification, are the ones in which we can place the most confidence. These reliable facts have achieved a broad and deep consensus within their respective fields of interest. As the philosopher Mary Midgley said, "facts are data—material which, for purposes of a particular enquiry, does not need to be reconsidered."[39] In other words, a fact in any realm of human enquiry amounts to a discussion frozen in time, halted where a particular line of enquiry has come to a standstill, for want of further data or new insight.

From the perspective of critical moral realism, basic value judgments such as "genocide is bad" or "altruism is good" are categorical. Value judgements are more than just emotional responses: the term "good" refers to an objective property. The statement "it is good" expresses not just an attitude, but a true-or-false judgement that can be verified by real-world observation and experience. For the moral realist, ethical claims are similar to statements like "the sky is blue." That is, such statements meet the same criteria of *fact* as material facts do. Assertions that "the

---

38 The distinction between realism and idealism is central to philosophy and is discussed in most introductory texts. Jacques Maritain was among the first to use the "critical" distinction in connection with realism in *Degrees of Knowledge* (Notre Dame: University of Notre Dame Press, 1995) and *A Preface to Metaphysics* (Salem: Ayer Company Publishers, 1987).

39 Mary Midgley, *Wisdom, Information and Wonder* (London: Routledge, 2001), 156.

disabled ought to be destroyed at birth," or that "adulterers ought to be stoned to death," or that "animals have no right to humane treatment," are quite as false as the statement that water flows uphill. Their falsity is not just a matter of somebody's opinion—it's a fact.

The equivalence of moral and material fact leads to the further conclusion that the commonplace notion of a dichotomy between fact and value—or more accurately, between moral and scientific fact—turns out to be fictitious. "The word fact, in its normal usage," Midgley says, "is not properly opposed to value, but to something more like conjecture or opinion." Neither is "superior" to the other. Both fact and value express knowledge that can be taken to the bank.

Furthermore, fact and value are unavoidably entangled with each other simply because human enquiry, including scientific observation, data collection, and computation, is always value-laden to some greater or lesser degree simply because it is undertaken by human beings. Nor can scientific realities be excluded from a conversation about values, if that dialogue is to have any practical application to the material world in which we live.

Why, then, do we continue to treat scientific and moral judgement as hermetic, unrelated areas of knowledge, as we do when we talk about fact/value distinctions? Perhaps for the reason suggested by philosopher Hilary Putnam:

> For one thing, it is much easier to say, "that's a value judgment," meaning, "that's just a matter of subjective preference," than to do what Socrates tried to teach us: to examine who we are and what our deepest convictions are and hold those convictions up to the searching test of reflective examination.... The worst thing about the fact/value dichotomy is that in practice it functions as a discussion-stopper, and not just a discussion-stopper, but a thought-stopper.[40]

The great chemist and philosopher of science Michael Polanyi (1891–1976) wrote, "in every judgement of scientific validity there ... remains implied the supposition that we accept the premises of science and that the scientist's conscience can be relied upon." No one can become a scientist, he says, "unless he presumes that the scientific

40 Hilary Putnam, *The Collapse of the Fact/Value Dichotomy and Other Essays* (Cambridge: Harvard University Press, 2002), 42.

doctrine and method are fundamentally sound and that their ultimate premises can be unquestioningly accepted." He or she must accept that reality is so constructed that its qualities are accessible to human reason, and that the scientific method of enquiry is sound.

Polanyi notes parenthetically that when these conditions are met, "we have … an instance of the process described epigrammatically by the Christian Church Fathers in the words: *fides quaerens intellectum*, faith in search of understanding." Put another way, any attempt to understand must be sustained by a belief, a faith, that there is something there that can be understood. *This applies equally to science and moral enquiry.*

Although it takes faith to persist in the pursuit of truth, the truth or falsity of a statement of fact, either moral or scientific, is not to be judged ultimately by how well it fits with some theoretical, *a priori* assumption or dogma. However, these may lurk in the background, for instance as a belief in the real existence of good, or in the ability of human reason to comprehend nature's workings. For humans, with our finite intellectual capacity, the truth and reliability of statements of fact depend, instead, on a network of prior knowledge linking the statement we want to verify with others of the same kind that have their own network of evidence. It depends ultimately on "the whole map of our experience and of the world which we believe to surround us."[41]

And so, in the end, the body of fact that makes up our total understanding of the world is like a vast crossword puzzle, in which having the correct answer to the clue for *fourteen Across* may depend on knowing the correct answer to *three Down*, and so on until the puzzle is complete. Reality, though, is for all practical purposes infinite, and so the puzzle is never done. And as long as that's the case it is always possible that an incorrect answer will be discovered deep in the matrix, forcing reconsideration of every other related answer, in principle up to and including the whole puzzle.[42]

Putnam reinforces this point in arguing for the factual nature of moral knowledge:

> It is possible to do science without supposing that one needs a metaphysical foundation for the enterprise. It is equally possible to live an ethical life

41 Midgley, *Wisdom*, 137.

42 An authoritative detailing of this approach to epistemology can be found in Susan Haack, *Evidence and Inquiry: Towards Reconstruction in Epistemology* (London: Blackwell, 1995).

> without supposing that one needs a metaphysical foundation.... As John Dewey noted long ago, the objectivity that ethical claims require is not the kind that is provided by Platonic or other foundation that is there in advance of our engaging in ethical life and ethical reflection; it is the ability to withstand the sort of criticism that arises in the problematic situations that we actually encounter.[43]

It is worth repeating that no fact in the modern scientific consensus on the nature of physical reality is more than about 450 years old, while consensus on moral issues such as truth, justice, equity, and human dignity often stretches back to the beginnings of recorded history. It is also noteworthy that when shifts in moral consensus occur—i.e., when slavery is abolished, or torture is outlawed, or the right of animals to humane treatment is recognized, or women's suffrage is enacted—they tend to have a much more significant impact on daily life than even a genuine scientific revolution like the displacement of Newton's physics by Einstein's relativity. And like Kant's categorical imperatives, they tend to be immune to revision.

The claim, then, is that both moral and scientific facts are ultimately established by *consensus*, and the more widespread and enduring that consensus is, the more confidence we have in the knowledge. When a significant shift in that consensus occurs, we do not expect to go back to earlier views, especially where moral knowledge is concerned. We move ahead.

At the same time, however, the possibility of falsification is never completely extinguished. If the moral realists are correct, as I believe they are, then it is crucial that moral fact be integrated into the formal matrix of knowledge so that the two categories of fact—both tested sources of knowledge—support one another, creating a more robust and resilient structure, one that is less likely to conceal catastrophic flaws and reliably reflects reality in all its complexity. It might be called wisdom.

---

43 Putnam, *The Collapse of the Fact/Value Dichotomy*, 94.

4. Biology and Good

If we can accept that good is part of the primordial order of things, folded in like gravity, then we must accept that humanity is necessarily in some way aligned with or touched by good, and that we are all susceptible to its influence. How could it be otherwise? We are all stardust, and just as we are sensitive to gravity and other unseen natural phenomena, we must in some sense be influenced by good, and shaped by it.

As we've seen, good is not just a metaphysical or theoretical concept: it is a discoverable and verifiable element of reality. Certainly, we are able to sense good and to know it when we see it. We have various names for this ability including "conscience," "moral sense," "moral compass," or the "moral impulse" within us. Biologist Marc Hauser concludes in his landmark study *Moral Minds* that,

> We are endowed with a moral acquisition device. Infants are born with the building blocks for making sense of the causes and consequences of actions, and their early capacities grow and interface with others to generate moral judgments. Infants are also equipped with a suite of unconscious, automatic emotions that can reinforce the expression of some actions while blocking others. Together, these capacities enable children to build moral systems.[44]

[44] Marc Hauser, *Moral Minds: The Nature of Right and Wrong* (New York: Harper Perennial, 2006).

Aristotle said something very similar: "Neither by nature, then, nor contrary to nature do the virtues arise in us; rather we are adapted by nature to receive them and are made perfect by habit."[45]

Eight centuries later, the great Catholic theologian and philosopher Saint Augustine of Hippo (354–430 CE) was grappling with the mysteries of this faculty when he concluded that morality is the product of charity, which is the *pondus*—the attractive force—of love that draws us to "that which we ought to love." Immanuel Kant in the eighteenth century confessed to being awed by two things: "the starry heavens above me and the mystery of the moral law within me." Contemporary thinkers like Noam Chomsky and John Rawls speak of our innate moral grammar.

Try this thought experiment:[46]

> *Fact*: We are, like everything else in the universe, products of the Big Bang. We are composed of the same basic materials and subject to the same fundamental forces as the stars.
>
> *Consider:* You're at home reading a book; you feel thirsty. You get up and pour yourself a glass of water and drink it. The water drains into your stomach, and from there seeps into your bloodstream, into cells, eventually reaching your brain. There, *the water begins to think*.
>
> *Reflect*: Are we the universe thinking? Put more broadly, is consciousness itself an inherently moral phenomenon, as Aristotle and Augustine suggest? Is consciousness in some sense oriented toward the good?

Thomas Hobbes saw human beings in their natural state as innately savage, brutishly self-interested, and focused solely on self-preservation. He said we were able to build stable societies only when war-weariness and fear for our personal security led us to consent to domination by an absolute ruler. But the evidence presented in the previous chapter suggests something very different. It is not terror, but our innate moral

---

45 Aristotle, *Nicomachean Ethics,* Book 2:1, 1003a. in W. D. Ross (trans,), *Aristotle* (New York, Meridian Books, 1959).

46 I have borrowed this illustration from physicist and cosmologist Brian Swimme.

sensibility that spurs us to look for ways to make our world a better, more just, and convivial place. We do this by building those social, political, legal, and economic institutions that define civilization.[47]

This is not the evolutionary discipline proposed as the basis for moral behaviour by David Hume (1711–76), who argued that social cooperation proved to be so important to survival that it eventually became embedded in the human psyche in principles such as justice. For Hume, morality was therefore a product of the course of human history. For the moral realist, Good is instead an aspect of the world's fundamental makeup.

As sociologist Zygmunt Bauman writes,

> Moral responsibility ... is the first reality of the self, a starting point rather than a product of society. It precedes all engagement with the Other, be it through knowledge, evaluation, suffering or doing. It has therefore no "foundation"—no cause, no determining factor.... [T]here is no self before the moral self, morality being the ultimate, non-determined presence, indeed an act of creation *ex nihilo*, if ever there was one.

The idea is by now familiar: morality as the human expression of good reflects the natural, numinous order of things ("natural" as opposed to supernatural, "numinous" in that it is not (yet) fully explainable within the framework of conventional science).

As is the case with the pull of gravity, or the passage of time, or the mystery of consciousness—those other everyday imponderables that we can identify but not fully explain—we do not need to understand the origin and genealogy of good to be able to study it profitably. We can accept it as an indisputable phenomenon of which we are aware through both observation (i.e., through our senses) and through intuition and introspection.

In other words, good is part of what is sometimes called the phenomenological world: the world that precedes formal, organized knowledge; the world that is addressed by such knowledge. Good therefore can be studied philosophically as a concept, but it can also be studied in a traditionally "scientific" way as suggested earlier.

---

[47] Zygmunt Bauman, *Postmodern Ethics* (Oxford: Blackwell Publishers, 1993) 13.

As the scientist does, the moral enquirer will begin with a hypothesis and go on to propose formal experiments and organized observations, the purpose of which is to challenge the hypothesis by testing it against phenomenological evidence. Those conjectures are most reliable and secure when successfully, in repeated tests, they remain unfalsified and therefore viable, and in that sense factual or true.

The hypothesis of an innate moral grammar could be seen as one such success story. Psychologist Steven Pinker writes that, in his discipline's exploration of morality and the moral sense now widely conceded to exist, "moral intuitions are being drawn out of people in the lab, on Web sites and in brain scanners, and are being explained with tools from game theory, neuroscience and evolutionary biology." The result, he says, has been that "the human moral sense turns out to be an organ of considerable complexity, with quirks that reflect its evolutionary history and its neurobiological foundations."[48] For example, psychologists have established that an individual's moral reactions to a given situation are typically immediate and powerful, but people frequently have trouble explaining why they responded in the way they did.

Another prominent psychologist, Jonathan Haidt, has concluded that when it comes to their lives as moral agents, people generally do not think moral problems through in a logical way, but rather provide after-the-fact rationalizations for conclusions that seem to be arrived at unconsciously, intuitively, or instinctively.[49] Like Hume 250 years earlier, Haidt imagines that what we describe as moral behaviour is a product of evolution, focusing on survival through the benefits of group loyalties. Reason is engaged only as a literal "afterthought," to justify our impulsive actions. We defend our tribe's values not because they make sense, but because we have been trained to do so through the long history of human evolution. He describes the moral person as a rational being riding an emotional elephant: the elephant can be nudged but is mostly in charge. What is "good" behaviour in an authentically moral and ethical sense is left for the rational mind to decide.

The continuing search for biological causes of moral behaviour has been taken up by the cognitive neuroscientist Joshua Greene and colleagues at

---

[48] Steven Pinker, "The Moral Instinct," *New York Times*, January 13, 2008.

[49] Jonathan Haidt, *The Righteous Mind* (London: Vintage, 2013) and other work.

Princeton University, who have watched blood-flow functions on M.R.I. brain scanners as subjects are asked to respond to various moral dilemmas presented to them.[50] The researchers have established that areas of the brain known to be involved in emotional responses are invariably among the regions active in moral decision-making. Where those emotion-related regions of the brain have been damaged, they found, subjects are apt to make decisions on strictly utilitarian grounds. So that, for example, they would see no dilemma in whether a surgeon should or should not kill a comatose but otherwise healthy patient in order to harvest her organs to save one or more dying patients whose achievements and future potential for doing good in the world are unimpeachable. For these subjects, the simple utilitarian numbers—the calculation of happiness created versus pain caused—would make the decision an obvious one. What do we learn about true morality from this neurophysiological research? Or from the speculations of evolutionary psychologists like Pinker and Haidt and their colleagues? Not much.

The brain states measured by the scientist, like the motivating impulses reported by psychologists' survey respondents, represent the *material conditions* for whatever *thought* is going on in the subject. The thought itself—whether or not the expression of some evolutionary "learning" process—is quite another thing, so that what the neurologist knows while observing her instruments or the psychologist learns from tabulating survey results, and what the subject knows while thinking, are not all the same. Experiments like these are classic reductionist science. While they may inform us that emotion is involved in making moral judgments, they tell us next to nothing about morality itself. The fact that the brain responds in specific and identifiable ways to moral challenges merely raises the question of whether electro-chemical brain states determine thought, or vice-versa. Most scientists prefer to think the former, of course, because that allows them to conduct experiments and collect numerical data. But this seems to be an unjustifiable position. After all, the entire premise of psychotherapy and related "talk-therapy" disciplines is that thought can alter chemical brain states—indeed, there is much evidence that thought can alter physiology throughout the body. This has been well-demonstrated, for example, in yogic healing

[50] Laura Helmuth, "Emotions are Rationale for Some Moral Dilemmas," *Science*, September 13, 2001.

disciplines and in recent medical discoveries in brain plasticity and the ability of thoughts to repair brain damage.[51]

It would seem clear, according to the best evidence available to us, both moral and scientific, that we can safely assign the existence of an innate moral sensibility in human beings to the "fact" column. The fabled and uncannily reliable "moral compass" exists. And by the logic of necessity, good itself must also exist.

What, then, of that other burning issue raised by Hobbes and his rationalist friends, the incorrigibly selfish essence of human nature. It is an assumption worth re-examining because, as we'll see later, it is an article of faith in modern economics and other social sciences. And of course, it is central to any discussion of morality and moral agents. The question being posed is: are humans essentially (though perhaps not exclusively) self-interested, or are we essentially (though perhaps not exclusively) altruistic? Are we essentially competitive, or are we more cooperative and collaborative by nature? ("Essentially" here should be understood in the sense of what is fundamental to our nature, a defining characteristic of our makeup.)

The relatively new science of evolutionary biology has attempted to make room for enquiry into the nature of morality within this characteristically reductionist discipline. It has done so by attempting to show that even though Darwin's model of natural selection through competition for scarce resources clearly operates on the basis of self-interest (i.e., each organism doing what's best for its survival), it is still possible for an individual organism such as a human being to behave in ways that appear to be authentically altruistic, or other-directed. That is, to participate in other-directed activity, expecting no hidden or explicit reward.

Darwin himself found the presence of morality in humans difficult to understand, given our evolution from a "hairy, tailed quadruped." In a long chapter devoted to the topic in *The Descent of Man* (1871) he argued that our apparent other-directedness is an evolutionary trait common to social creatures. This trait, he believed, evolved in two stages. First, through the need to nurture the young in birds and then in mammals (since neglected young do not survive). Second, as humans gain intellectual capacity, they are able to reflect on their own past behaviour and that of others, and form judgements based on the results. This, in turn, led to the development of a conscience: "the supreme judge and monitor" of behaviour.

51 See, for example, Moheb Costandi, *Neuroplasticity* (Cambridge: MIT Press, 2016).

A modern socio-biologist might describe the process like this: natural selection leads to the dominance of organisms that favour tit-for-tat behaviour, because it serves their survival interests better than pure selfishness. "You scratch my back and I'll scratch yours" is a sound survival strategy, and, indeed, is widely practised even among non-human animals.[52] That's called "reciprocal altruism," and it needs to be distinguished from true altruism in which there is no expectation of reward, or to put in another way, in which a cost is incurred but no benefit is expected in return.

A growing number of anthropologists and economists have accepted a modified version of the theory of reciprocal altruism as a description of a uniquely human evolutionary adaptation, refining it slightly as "strong reciprocity." This is described as a tendency within groups for individuals to cooperate with others, and seek out and punish those who don't follow the rules of cooperation. Although strong reciprocity is not overtly selfish, it is strategic. The intent of the punishment is not to convert, but to drive the cheaters out. Successful adaptation means "focusing our cooperative efforts on those who are trustworthy," (and therefore likely to reciprocate).[53]

As ingenious as this theory of the biological origins of moral behaviour may be—and regardless of whether it seems even remotely plausible—it still has nothing whatever to say about the nature of morality itself. Transferred to the human realm, it leaves fundamental questions unanswered. For example, what is it that makes cheating immoral (and not just bad strategy)?

Morality cannot simply be a matter of survival technique. One can imagine any number of circumstances in which good survival strategy is also immoral, such as stealing a child's life jacket to keep oneself afloat in a shipwreck. And why do we honour the individual who sacrifices herself for the child by doing the opposite?

In the real world we all inhabit, self-sacrifice without recompense is a feature of behaviour we see routinely and consider to be highly virtuous. However, evolutionary theory brings us no closer to answering Socrates's question: What is good? What is virtuous conduct? Early in the history of moral philosophy Plato posed a question that is directly relevant to issues of biological necessity and human behaviour. Appearing in a

52 Robert Trivers, "The Evolution of Reciprocal Altruism," *Quarterly Review of Biology*, 46 (March 1971): 35–57.

53 Hauser, *Moral Minds*.

dialogue between Socrates and a man named Euthyphro, this question is remembered as the Euthyphro dilemma.

The two are discussing the nature of piety, of reverence for the gods. Socrates asks: is something good because it is favoured by the gods? Or does the fact the gods favour something *make* it good? In terms of modern religious debate, the question becomes one of crucial significance since God's will is seen as the foundation of ethics—God determines what is good and what is not. This is known as divine command theory. (How one comes to know God's will is a complicating issue that we need not deal with here: generally, it is knowledge acquired through divinely-inspired texts, testimony of the saintly, or prayer.)

The Euthyphro dilemma challenges divine command theory by asking whether morally good acts are morally good because they are acts that have been willed by God, or does God will the acts because they are morally good? Problems arise either way. If whatever God wills must be, by definition, morally good, then the question of what is moral is emptied of rational meaning, becoming tautological: how do we know an action is good? Because God wills it. Why does God will it? Because it's good. This leaves the aspiring human with little to cling to by way of practical guidance. To escape the tautology, it would be necessary to imagine God calling on some prior, transcendent notion of morality, an idea which, in religious terms, is nonsensical.

Brought further up to date into the realms of sociobiology, evolutionary biology, and biological explanations for altruism, the same kinds of objections apply—the Euthyphro dilemma remains. Plainly stated: can any biologically ordained preference whatsoever justify a claim of moral or immoral behaviour? If science were to discover a gene for racism, would we then be justified in becoming racists, commanded by our genetic inheritance? Or if it were to be firmly established that eons of evolutionary adaptation have conditioned us to see selfish behaviour as moral, would we be justified in abandoning aspirations to altruism? The answer in both cases has to be: of course not. Where does "of course not" come from? It can't be a biologically determined response because that would mean we are biologically determined to be both racist and not-racist, egoistic and altruistic, which is nonsense. So, the moral judgement behind "of course not" must be rooted elsewhere.

Let us leave the last word to Aristotle and his perennial, practical wisdom. For Aristotle, the science of moral living, the highest of all disciplines, is the study of politics. It would be foolish to suggest that his prescriptions for good governance ought to be adopted in the contemporary world, or even that they are capable of being adapted to our much more complex situation. But they do have value as a sounding board—as great, eternal ideas against which others can be measured and weighed. Contemporary thinkers may have ideas of more direct application to today's situation, but we want to get back to basics here, for the very good reason that we have evidently lost sight of the kinds of important fundamental realities that so concerned the ancients.

What we learn from Aristotle is that morality, while it is ultimately rooted in a universal good (as Plato argued), is nonetheless a matter for local interpretation, and therefore it is, in its detailed application, a social enterprise. The moral individual must be well-versed in these real-life distinctions. It follows that no person can hope to lead a virtuous life without being embedded from childhood in a moral community. While we may emerge from the womb equipped with a basic, universal moral grammar, the way it is articulated depends on our community. Without community involvement, it may not develop at all.

For Aristotle, the individual can find ultimate fulfilment only in the community, which, for him, was the city-state. This is because being a moral person and doing good are one in the same: morality is a matter of action within a social environment. One can be stuffed with moral theory and abstract ethical ideas, but to *be* a moral person one must make real moral choices and act on them. Morality, which is subsumed by the science of politics, is a *practical* science in that its study is not one of theory, but of action.

We are all moral creatures, Aristotle believed. We are born with a moral foundation, but the only way for a young person to learn to be moral in practice—to learn moral *behaviour*—is to observe the actions of moral persons in her or his community. Political science will be able to discover true moral universals through the study of what various communities consider to be moral behaviour, but while theoretical education can be helpful, it is not essential to becoming a moral person, he believed. The key to morality in both the individual and the community is upbringing and early familiarity with the watchwords of morality—the *seemly* (or virtuous), and the *just*. "It makes no small difference, then whether we form [moral] habits of one kind or another from our very youth; it makes a very great difference, or rather *all* the difference," he insisted.[54]

The implication of this for governance, in Aristotle, is that the best state is one in which the young are raised from an early age to understand the complexities of moral behaviour. Morality can only exist in any useful sense if it is woven into the very fabric of the life of the state. Our contemporary idea of the ethics "expert"—who boasts specialized knowledge and strategies that can be applied like cosmetic surgery to morally problematic situations—is not one of which Aristotle would have approved. Nor would he have looked favourably on the rationalist notion that moral outcomes can automatically be generated by institutions whose optimal performance depends on fundamentally vicious, self-interested behaviour by individuals.

In Aristotle we are introduced to the idea that good can be more than an abstract perfection, a benchmark—that it is also what is good *for us*. Virtue is its own reward, certainly, but, for Aristotle, the virtuous person is also a happy person. Virtuous motivation, continuously exercised in action, is what makes a virtuous person, and what makes a person virtuous.

---

[54] *Entelecheia*, II, 1,1103b 23–25 (c. 350 BCE), in W. D. Ross (trans,), *Aristotle* (New York, Meridian Books, 1959).

5. The Birth of the Modern

An abiding concern for Enlightenment thinkers like David Hume, Denis Diderot, and the Paris *philosophes* was that rationalism, for all its dazzling new insights, was undermining the traditional Christian sources of moral discipline without providing a replacement. That worry was addressed when a satisfyingly scientific substitute for the guidance of the Church's moral dogma was found in the most surprising of places: in an embryonic theory of commercial enterprise and economic production, a new social science that would come to be called economics.

To understand how an arena of activity awash in such materialist objectives as profit, production, and wealth could be seen as embodying a kind of natural moral order, it helps to look back to the source code as represented in theorists like Francis Bacon and René Descartes, and the polymath philosopher Baruch Spinoza (an associate of Thomas Hobbes).

Born into a Jewish community in Amsterdam and educated there in the ferment of radical Enlightenment thinking, Spinoza's religious observance fell into neglect. He was excommunicated by his community in part for his pantheistic views on the nature of God, as well as his rejection of literal interpretations of Scripture. To support his intellectual pursuits, he learned the craft of lens grinding and was thus immersed in the burgeoning new science of optics. Indeed, it is thought that the silica dust from this work grinding lenses led to his death from lung disease in early middle age.

Like most of his fellow rationalists, Spinoza did not deny the existence of God, but he identified God with nature, using the terms interchangeably. His naturalized God was perfect and had no needs or desires. In the perfect universe He created, embodied, and actualized, everything happened for a reason. Given this definition and given that his perfect God had no needs or desires, prescriptions for good behaviour could not logically be a product of any divine mandate.[55]

For Spinoza, ethical questions of good and bad were related not to any divine commands, but to what was good or bad for the individual person—to what promoted or impeded the individual's welfare or happiness. Spinoza's viewpoint became notorious: "Nothing happens in nature," he asserted, "which might be attributed to any defect in it." That is, the world as we find it is perfection, and everything that happens in nature fulfills a necessary purpose.[56] That being the case, he reasoned, it is a sign of ignorance to describe some actions as good and others wicked. The only appropriate definition of good, he said, is simply "that which we certainly know to be useful to us."[57]

Spinoza held that, using reason and the newly-implemented processes of scientific enquiry, the purposes of each of the human "passions" (we would say "drives" or emotions) would soon be deciphered, and understanding human relationships would then be no more challenging than calculating the motions of the planets. The proper, rational, attitude to so-called human vices—lust, gluttony, greed, and so on—was not to condemn them, he said, but to learn their purpose, because they certainly *had* a purpose in the overall scheme of things since "nothing happens in nature which might be attributed to any defect in it."

---

55 See the Euthyphro dilemma, Ch. 3 above. Spinoza resolves it by erasing it with his conception of God.

56 In this he was in accord with his contemporary, the great philosopher-mathematician Gottfried Wilhelm Leibniz (1646–1716), who had the misfortune to be unfairly ridiculed in Voltaire's famous satirical novella *Candide* (1759) as the relentlessly optimistic Professor Pangloss, who teaches his pupils that they live in "the best of all possible worlds," and that "all is for the best."

57 Spinoza, *Ethics*, 1677. By "useful" he meant conducive to the attaining of pleasure, but his definition of pleasure was very specific. Pleasure, he believed, was to be found in reliable knowledge of the world and of oneself, knowledge that is necessary to self-fulfilment. Pain, on the other hand, he defined as whatever gets in the way of attaining that knowledge and fulfilment. The highest forms of learning, he said, bring their possessor a blessedness, and peace of mind, because possessing such knowledge amounts to a discovering of the mind of God within oneself, and a contented acceptance of the deterministic nature of the world.

As an early and vigorous advocate of secularism, Spinoza decried the dominant influence of religion, particularly Protestant Christianity, on European society and its governments. He deplored the power and influence of clerics of all stripes and the ceremonial trappings they had contrived. He saw Scripture, both Jewish and Christian, as historical documents written by ordinary men and subject to corruption through repeated copying and translation over the centuries. He was an ethical egoist, who believed that it was a moral obligation always to choose those actions which maximize good for oneself. Doing so, he believed, would automatically promote the welfare of humanity at large.[58]

As shocking as it seemed at the time, Spinoza's radical view of good as "that which is certainly useful to us" was to be incorporated (stripped of its deistic subtleties) into the economic thinking that was emerging in Europe around what we now call liberal capitalism. This new ideology located the source of human well-being in economic behaviour as it is moulded by the competitive dynamics of the market economy. It would quickly become a fertile field of study which, as Spinoza had urged, took prominent human vices—such as self-interest, competitiveness, envy, and greed—and sought to explain their utility, in this case, in terms of business and commerce and their roles in advancing the common good.

Another theorizer representative of the times was the French theologian Pierre Nicole (1625–1695), whose tract *Of Charity and Self-Love* (1675) ruminated on the mechanics of the emerging capitalist market in France and elsewhere. Nicole argued that:

> By the means and help of ... commerce all necessaries for this life are supplied without intermixing charity with it. So that in states where charity has no admittance, because true religion is banished there, men do not cease to live with as much peace, safety, and comfort, as if they lived in a Republic of Saints.

For Nicole, the market, though not a replacement for "true" morality, was an alternative and highly satisfactory way of producing the conditions for happiness through the enlightened management of self-interest.

---

[58] In Spinoza's thought, ethical egoism left plenty of room for altruism, since it is often the case that one's happiness is magnified by the happiness of others, and so selfless service to others can be both personally and ethically fulfilling.

The unsettling moral status of emerging modern capitalist economies was laid bare in a provocative way by Bernard Mandeville, a Dutch physician who settled in London in the late seventeenth century. His *Fable of the Bees*, a potboiler first published in 1705, typified the rationalist thinker's unflinching commitment to look at things as they really are, rather than as what they ought to be. It stirred up a storm of condemnation but was nevertheless widely influential. The essayist Samuel Johnson said that every young man of the time had a copy on his shelves, in the belief that it was a wicked book. At over four hundred lines, it is too long to reproduce here, but it begins as follows:

A spacious hive well stocked with bees,
That lived in luxury and ease;
And yet as famed for laws and arms,
As yielding large and early swarms;
Was counted the great nursery
Of sciences and industry …

These insects lived like men, and all
Our actions they performed in small:
They did whatever's done in town,
And what belongs to sword, or gown:
Though the artful works, by nimble slight;
Of minute limbs, escaped human sight

Yet we've no engines; labourers,
Ships, castles, arms, artificers,
Craft, science, shop, or instrument,
But they had an equivalent …

It was vice, and the satisfaction of its demands, that made their economy flourish. Mandeville continues,

… The root of evil, Avarice,
That damned ill-natured baneful vice,
Was slave to Prodigality.
That noble sin; whilst Luxury
Employed a million of the poor,
And odious Pride a million more:

Envy itself, and Vanity,
Were ministers of industry;
Their darling folly, Fickleness
In diet, furniture, and dress
That strange ridiculous vice, was made
The very wheel that turned the trade …

Such were the blessings of that state;
Their crimes conspired to make 'em great;
And virtue, which from politics
Had learned a thousand cunning tricks,
Was, by their happy influence,
Made friends with vice: And ever since
The worst of all the multitude
Did something for the common good.

Mandeville's thesis was that virtue is nothing but hypocrisy, a sham idea introduced by rulers and philosophers of old as a propaganda tool for simplifying governance. In fact, said Mandeville, virtue is detrimental to the causes of commercial and intellectual progress, for it is the vices—the selfish, greedy, lustful impulses of people—that lead to the circulation of the wealth and capital that support luxurious living, which in turn enriches society and encourages cultural and intellectual activity.

The absence of self-interest is the death of progress, says Mandeville, and in his *Fable* he sketches what happens when the hive is one day smitten with righteousness, "blest with content[ment] and honesty." It falls into apathy and economic paralysis and is quickly depopulated. Mandeville writes:

As Pride and Luxury decrease,
So by degrees [traders] leave the seas,
Not merchants now; but companies
Remove whole manufacturies.
All arts and crafts neglected lie;
Content the bane of industry,
Makes 'em admire their homely store,
And neither seek, nor covet more …

In a concluding commentary on his poem, Mandeville minces no words when he explains that:

> After this I flatter myself to have demonstrated that neither the friendly qualities and affections that are natural to man, nor the real virtues he is capable of acquiring by reason and self-denial are the foundations of society; but that what we call evil in this world, moral as well as natural, is the grand principle that makes us sociable creatures, the solid basis, the life and support of all trades and employments without exception: That there we must look for the true origin of all arts and sciences, and that the moment evil ceases, the society must be spoiled if not totally dissolved.[59]

Wickedness, in other words, was actually a necessary precursor and helpmate to good. It is an idea Spinoza would have applauded.

The Irish satirist Jonathan Swift, an Anglican cleric, commented memorably on the rationalist, value-agnostic approach to economic thought in his notorious 1729 pamphlet, "A Modest Proposal: For Preventing the Children of Poor People in Ireland from Being a Burden to Their Parents or Country, and for Making Them Beneficial to the Publick." After describing at some length the miserable plight of the poor and starving in Ireland, Swift presents as a perfectly rational economic strategy a plan to solve the problem, by treating children born into poverty as a readily-available food source for the landed gentry:

> I have been assured by a very knowing American of my acquaintance in London, that a young healthy child well nursed, is, at a year old, a most delicious nourishing and wholesome food, whether stewed, roasted, baked, or boiled; and I make no doubt that it will equally serve in a fricassee, or a ragout.

Viciously lampooning value-neutral economic science, Swift uses statistical analysis to build an iron-clad demonstration of the utter futility of more conventional, less "rational" social welfare approaches to the alleviation of poverty and hunger.[60]

---

59 Bernard Mandeville, *The Fable of the Bees: Or Private Vices, Publick Benefits* (New York, Penguin Classics, 1989).

60 Jonathan Swift, "A Modest Proposal," in *The Broadview Anthology of English Literature: The Restoration and the 18th Century* (Peterborough: Broadview Press, 2009), 418. Here is another excerpt from this text, which further exemplifies Swift's tenor: "The number of souls in this kingdom being usually reckoned one million and a half, of these

Swift concludes his pamphlet with a withering nod to the values of scientific objectivity:

> I profess, in the sincerity of my heart, that I have not the least personal interest in endeavoring to promote this necessary work, having no other motive than the public good of my country, by advancing our trade, providing for infants, relieving the poor, and giving some pleasure to the rich. I have no children by which I can propose to get a single penny; the youngest being nine years old, and my wife past childbearing.[61]

Ouch. The contrast between the cool reasonableness of the satire and its outrageous moral implications places in painfully sharp focus the shortcomings of an economic science that strives to synthesize moral outcomes, and which reduces people to commodities in the process.

But by now the power and influence of the Roman Catholic Church was waning, and popular Protestant notions of individualism and human liberties had taken hold. Wealth and economic power were accruing to a rising class of capitalist entrepreneurs and traders, and in relatively short order the idea of a market economy in which prosperity is driven by intense, self-interested competition would push aside the medieval idea

---

I calculate there may be about two hundred thousand couples whose wives are breeders; from which number I subtract thirty thousand couples who are able to maintain their own children, although I apprehend there cannot be so many, under the present distresses of the kingdom; but this being granted, there will remain an hundred and seventy thousand breeders. I again subtract fifty thousand for those women who miscarry, or whose children die by accident or disease within the year. There only remains one hundred and twenty thousand children of poor parents annually born. The question therefore is, how this number shall be reared and provided for, which, as I have already said, under the present situation of affairs, is twenty thousand may be reserved for breed[ing], whereof only one-fourth part to be males; which is more than we allow to sheep, black cattle or swine; and my reason is, that these children are seldom the fruits of marriage, a circumstance not much regarded by our savages, therefore one male will be sufficient to serve four females. That the remaining hundred thousand may, at a year old, be offered in the sale to the persons of quality and fortune through the kingdom; always advising the mother to let them suck plentifully in the last month, so as to render them plump and fat for a good table. A child will make two dishes at an entertainment for friends; and when the family dines alone, the fore or hind quarter will make a reasonable dish, and seasoned with a little pepper or salt will be very good boiled on the fourth day, especially in winter."

61 Ibid, 419. See also George Wittkowsky, "Swift's Modest Proposal: The Biography of an Early Georgian Pamphlet," *Journal of the History of Ideas* 4, no. 1 (January 1943).

of commercial activity as a necessary evil, one that needed to be kept under strict control.

For a thousand years and more the moral teachings of the Catholic Church had treated the pursuit of wealth as a moral hazard. It interfered with the real business of life, which was to follow virtue, practise charity, strive for self-knowledge, and seek salvation. Where participation in business and commerce were unavoidable, the rules of morality were to be followed just as in all other aspects of life.

Self-interest and avarice were passions that needed careful repression. As R. H. Tawney writes in his classic *Religion and the Rise of Capitalism*:

> There is no place in medieval theory for economic activity which is not related to moral ends, and to found a science of society upon the assumption that the appetite for economic gain is a constant and measurable force, to be accepted, like other natural forces, as an inevitable and self-evident *datum*, would have appeared to the medieval thinker as hardly less irrational or less immoral than to make the premise of social philosophy the unrestrained operation of such necessary human attributes as pugnacity or the sexual instinct.[62]

But this is precisely what the rationalist ideology of Hobbes, Spinoza, Mandeville, and their contemporaries would accomplish—the founding of a science of society upon competition, self-interest, and an appetite for material gain.

The idea that the amenities and satisfactions of civilization are really a product of vice, and that for good to flourish we must encourage what is worst rather than best in humanity is, on the face of it, perverse. It would take some of the leading thinkers of the eighteenth and nineteenth centuries to convince us that it was nevertheless true, to make sense of it in a way we continue to accept to this day.

Voltaire, the celebrated French novelist, poet, and playwright, and one of rationalism's leading exponents, was the worst nightmare for conservative medieval moralists. It was a role he revelled in with pornographic glee as he penned *Candide*, in which the virtuous hero finds his moral scruples do not serve him well in a world made in the image of rationalist economic theory. For Voltaire, self-interest was, "the foundation of commerce, the

---

62 R.H. Tawney, *Religion and the Rise of Capitalism* (London: Penguin 1924, 1966), 43–4.

eternal link between men." While God had the option of "creating beings solely concerned with the good of others ... [He] has ordained things differently. Let us not condemn the instinct He has given us, and let us put it to the use He commands."[63] Here, with the precision of a great writer, is encapsulated the heart and soul of Enlightenment thought as it is found in the ideology of liberal market capitalism.

In Adam Smith's *The Wealth of Nations* (1776)—the canonic text of the new economic science—the necessary equilibrium of supply and demand organized by the "invisible hand" regulates human life and death in a way that is uncomfortably akin to Swift's scandalous lampoon. "The demand for men, *like any other commodity*," Smith says:

> ... necessarily regulates the production of men. Every species of animals naturally multiplies in proportion to their means of subsistence—[thus] among the inferior ranks of people the scantiness of subsistence sets limits to their reproduction—[which] it can do with no other way than by destroying a great part of their children.[64]

To the liberal capitalist market, even children have no "value" if they become a surplus commodity.

Joseph Townsend (1739–1816), an English cleric and dabbler in economic theory, railed against government welfare measures for the poor. "The poor know little of the motives which stimulate the higher ranks to action—pride, honour, and ambition." Therefore, he continued:

> The wisest legislator will never be able to devise a more equitable, a more effectual, nor in any respect a more suitable punishment, than hunger is for the disobedient servant. Hunger will tame the fiercest animals, it will teach decency and civility, obedience and subjection to the most brutish, the most obstinate, and the most perverse.... When hunger is either felt or feared, the desire of obtaining bread will quietly dispose the mind to undergo the greatest hardships, and will sweeten the severest labours.[65]

---

63 Voltaire, *Lettres philosophiques (Letters on the English)*, 1734.

64 Adam Smith, *The Wealth of Nations* (Digireads E-book, 2009), 50. Emphasis added.

65 Joseph Townsend, "A Dissertation on the Poor Laws, By a Well-Wisher to Mankind" 1786 (Los Angeles, University of California Press, 1971, p. 16).

From the vantage point of the twenty-first century's digital world, we can see that what Smith and the early market economists were doing was laying the groundwork for a set of algorithms or formal rules that would describe and help to govern the operations of an increasingly complex economic environment. The new algorithms would be legal and regulatory, and designed to ensure the optimal operation of natural law. Once in place, those mechanizing rules would make possible the continuous fine-tuning necessary to maximize output and minimize direct costs within the system. Efficiency was the goal; autonomy a requirement. Equity, it was assumed, would follow.

6. Mechanizing Virtue: The Fabulous Free Market

A story is told of the early childhood of Adam Smith, the godfather of modern market capitalism, that is breathtaking in its latent potential for history. In 1727, when he was four years old and visiting an uncle with his widowed mother in the Scottish fishing village of Strathenry, Smith was abducted by a band of Roma tinkers. A pursuit was hastily mounted, and the young lad was abandoned by his captors and returned to his mother. An early Smith biographer, a man of wry humor, was no doubt accurate when he said that Smith "would have made, I fear, a poor gypsy."[66]

Like Hobbes before him, Smith at an early age became the beneficiary of the sponsorship of an aristocratic family, whose scion he was hired to tutor and with whom he journeyed to the continent for the mandatory Grand Tour. He was already acquainted with many of the prominent figures of the time on his side of the English Channel including chemist Joseph Black, James Watt of steam engine fame, businessman and merchant trader Andrew Cochrane, as well as the great philosopher David Hume. He would later establish friendships with political philosopher Edmund Burke, essayist Samuel Johnson, and historian Edward Gibbon. It is thought that he was also an acquaintance of Benjamin Franklin.

66 John Rae, *Life of Adam Smith* (London: Macmillan & Co., 1895). There are several versions of this story, as told by different biographers. See Stuart Kells, "Adam Smith, Kidnapped," *La Trobe University News*, Jan 23, 2020.

On the continent, Smith was to meet many of the leading lights of the so-called French Enlightenment. In Geneva, he conversed with Voltaire, and in Paris he mingled with a group of social reformers and theoreticians who called themselves *les* économistes, and who are known to history as the physiocrats.

The group's leader was court physician to Louis XV, François Quesnay, who is credited with writing the first systematic analysis of an entire economy. Steeped in the contemporary theories of natural law and natural justice (the term *physiocracy* means the rule of nature), Quesnay and the physiocrats also believed in a natural economic order. They were violently opposed to regulation, "inappropriate" taxation, and other forms of interference. Their famous watchword was "*Laissez faire, laissez passer.*" They proposed the elimination of all taxes except an *impôt unique* on the net income from land, which they regarded as the true source of all wealth. The precise extent of the physiocrats' influence on Smith's own economic thinking is controversial, but it is known that he was a sincere admirer of Quesnay, to whom he had intended to dedicate his own economic opus prior to the doctor's death.

Smith received a university education in moral philosophy at Glasgow and Oxford at a time when the discipline encompassed not only ethics and the fundamentals of religion, but also law and political economy. He came to see economics and ethics as being so closely related as to be inseparable, and he published landmark works in both fields.

The first of these was the *Theory of Moral Sentiments* (1759), which he wrote while teaching moral philosophy at Glasgow University. In it he outlines the principles of "human nature" which, in keeping with the thinking of his time, he took to be elements of natural law. From these principles, human behaviour and the workings of social institutions could be deduced, much as the trajectory of a missile can be predicted from physical data.

A central question addressed by the book is the origins of moral behaviour. Given what was alleged in contemporary thought to be an over-arching power of the instinctual drives of self-interest and self-preservation, how is it possible for people to make objective moral judgements on their own actions and those of others? How is it that morality remained a concern?

Smith's eventual answer is that each of us has within us an observer (today we would call it the superego) who acts as an "impartial spectator," observing, judging, and communicating through an inner voice that cannot be ignored. Less than entirely satisfying as a solution (indeed, we could enquire into the basis for the spectator's moral judgement) Smith's hypothesis would be disregarded by later rationalist and behaviourist thinkers, who preferred to ignore the question altogether as "metaphysical" and therefore nonsensical.

Nevertheless, Smith's perception of the dual nature of people—their compelling, instinctual passions on the one hand and their ability to reason and feel sympathy on the other—would provide the cornerstone of his later, enormously influential economic ideas. He theorized that the drives of passion were regulated and harnessed for good largely through rationally designed social institutions that served to channel aggressive, competitive "natural" instincts into socially beneficial outcomes. Self-interested people, he said, are in their public lives "led by an invisible hand ... without knowing it, without intending it, [to] advance the interest of the society."[67]

Smith published his masterwork, *The Wealth of Nations* (1776) on his return from Europe, two years after Voltaire's death, and a century after Spinoza had flourished. It was the same year in which British colonies in what is now known as the United States of America asserted their independence from Great Britain, with an historic Declaration redolent of Enlightenment ideas in its references to "Laws of Nature" and "self-evident" truths. In Smith's great treatise, the role of self-interest in creating public welfare is worked out in consummate detail. He began, as a good rationalist thinker would, from what he took to be an obvious and inarguable axiom. He writes,

> [M]an has almost constant occasion for the help of his brethren, and it is in vain for him to expect it from their benevolence only. He will be more likely to prevail if he can interest their self-love in his favour, and shew them that it is for their own advantage to do for him what he requires of them.... It is not through the benevolence of the butcher, the brewer or the baker that we expect our dinner, but from their regard to their own interests. We address ourselves, not to their humanity but to their self-love, and never talk to them of our own necessities but of their advantages. Nobody but a beggar chooses to depend chiefly upon the benevolence of his fellow citizens.[68]

[67] Adam Smith, *The Theory of Moral Sentiments*, Part IV, Chapter I, 184–5, para. 10. http://knarf.english.upenn.edu/Smith/tms124.html

[68] Adam Smith, *An Inquiry into the Nature and Causes of the Wealth of Nations*, ed. R. H. Campbell and A.S. Skinner (New York: Liberty Fund 1776, 1981), 346, para. 36.

Just like his earlier book, *Wealth of Nations* argued that social institutions channel human vice toward socially beneficent results. Both books assume, without much thought given to anthropological or historical evidence (which was in any case scanty), that social and economic relationships as they were presumed to exist in primitive society, are natural ecological phenomena. As such, it followed that these relationships function best when left alone. Government interference in economic institutions, even when in the pursuit of public good, is therefore misguided and likely to be self-defeating.

In its influence on individual entrepreneurs, the natural algorithmic operation of market capitalism with its rich competition was presumed by Smith to strongly discourage unethical or otherwise antisocial behaviour while at the same time reinforcing the "propriety" or discipline necessary to orderly commerce. In highlighting competition as the crucial institutional mechanism, Smith said, "the real and effectual discipline which is exercised over a workman ... is that of his customers. It is the fear of losing their employment [to competitors] which restrains his frauds and corrects his negligence."

Egoism, or self-interest, was the abiding passion of all people, he said, but the ruling classes were in the fortunate position of being able to freely indulge their greed. "They are themselves always, and without any exception, the greatest spendthrifts in the society," he maintained.[69] But Smith also recognized that there is a side to human nature that can be generous and sympathetic. As we've seen, he credited this to a feature of human psychology that he described as a built-in, impartial observer in each of us, a faculty similar to what most of us call a conscience, or perhaps, a moral compass. But this moral faculty was not nearly as effective in guiding human behaviour as the economic relations that

This extract is preceded by this less famous but revealing passage: "Nobody ever saw a dog make a fair and deliberate exchange of one bone or another with another dog.... When an animal wants to obtain something either of a man or of another animal, it has no other means of persuasion but to gain the favour of those whose service it requires. Man sometimes uses the same arts with his brethren, and when he has no other means of engaging them to act according to his Inclinations, endeavours by every servile and fawning attention to obtain their good will. He has not time, however, to do this upon every occasion. In civilized society he stands at all times in need of the cooperation and assistance of great multitudes, while his whole life is scarce sufficient to gain the friendship of a few persons."

[69] Adam Smith, *The Wealth of Nations*, Book II, Chapter III, 346, para. 36. Op. cit.

govern our lives as producers and consumers, landlords and merchants, manufacturers, farmers, labourers, and craftspeople. The dynamics or algorithms of the capitalist market economy, Smith believed, were a form of natural law, discovered rather than invented.

In retrospect, of course, we can see that the rules and conventions of economic exchange that emerged with the market capitalism of Smith's time are human inventions, frequently imposed through edict and the force of arms. Smith, however, saw in them God's benevolent hand guiding the affairs of humanity. In transactions of the marketplace, the individual person,

> ... intends only his own gain, and he is *in this, as in many other cases, led by an invisible hand* to promote an end which was no part of his intention. Nor is it always the worse for the society that it was no part of it. By pursuing his own interest he frequently promotes that of the society more effectually than when he really intends to promote it. I have never known much good done by those who affected to trade for the public good. It is an affection indeed, not very common among merchants, and very few words need to be employed in dissuading them from it.[70]

Much of *Wealth of Nations* is devoted to describing in detail how the "invisible hand" operates. Mutual competition among innately self-interested people, who are instinctively driven to barter and trade, constantly forces the prices of commodities down to their "natural" level, which is determined by the cost of production. Smith explained how wages and rents and profits, which are all costs of production, are each in their turn subject to competition, and therefore held to *their* "natural" levels.

Smith was anxious to explain how a steady expansion of wealth could occur within this self-regulating mechanism, and his explanation is both ingenious and dangerously flawed. When manufacturers who have accumulated capital wish to expand production, they hire on new workers. (Smith was writing just prior to the looming Industrial Revolution in Great Britain.) When they do this, they bid up wages, according to the law that says that increased demand for an existing supply means higher prices. All things being equal, the higher wages

---

70 Ibid, 264. (Emphasis added.)

ought to spell disaster for the manufacturers (since higher costs make them less competitive), but there is a loophole. Higher wages for workers increase their numbers (mainly, Smith presumed, through decreases in infant mortality that would come with improved living standards) and with more workers bidding against one another for jobs, wages fall. Profits and capital accumulation increase, and the cycle can repeat itself.

In this way, the economy could notch its way up, step by step, to a level where even those at the bottom of the economic ladder could be made relatively prosperous. The problem, not clearly visible for another century and a half, was that this theoretical dynamic worked only so long as growth was continuous. The issue of projecting infinite growth within a finite natural environment would begin to attract serious attention midway through the twentieth century.

Smith's analysis depicted a smoothly running, self-regulating machine. It was perfectly attuned to the mechanistic, deterministic mind-set of his age, in which natural law amounted to operating rules or algorithms whose origins might or might not be divine (a question that was anyway of little consequence for continuing human progress). The analysis also incorporated a concept his era had invented—that is, human *progress* through the application of reason. This was confidently described as a steady improvement in material living standards accompanying the ongoing human conquest of nature with the help of technology. Not much thought was given to ultimate goals or to defining "improvement," or even to establishing what is meant by standards of living. His theories constitute nothing less than the genesis of an ambitious program for the synthesis of moral behaviour to reinforce, if not replace, less reliable and increasingly ill-fitting religious moral codes with self-sustaining, self-regulating, algorithmic processes within institutions.

Smith's Newton-like formalization of contemporary economic practice was among the loftiest products of the exhilarating intellectual atmosphere of the early modern era, in which nothing seemed beyond rational, scientific explanation; no mystery unsolvable, no problem immune to human understanding and resolution.[71] When fused with

[71] Another highlight is the work of Smith's contemporary, the French political philosopher Claude Henri Saint-Simon (1769–1825). He saw a future in which politics would be replaced by scientifically-engineered institutions for transforming human irrationalities into rational behaviour, much as the capitalist market of Adam Smith transformed individual vice into collective well-being. Governance would be reduced to administration, to be undertaken by industrial leaders and scientists. His ideas for a technical meritocracy found favour, especially, with a new class of scientifically

the radical ideas of a new philosophy called utilitarianism and blended with Darwin's forthcoming theory of evolution, it would become the foundation upon which subsequent capitalist market theory has been built.

Revolutionary though his ideas may seem in retrospect, Smith was in some respects a dinosaur in the environment of intellectual ferment and experimentation in which he lived and worked. His Anglican piety and his acknowledgement of some residual altruism in people was out of step with the more ideologically flamboyant and outspoken rationalist thinkers, notably the utilitarian philosophers, all of whom moonlighted as economists. According to utilitarian theorist and jurist Jeremy Bentham (1743–1832), "human beings are deficient in altruism" and most of the time inclined to act in their own self-interest.[72] This fact made it necessary for a system of strict social regulation to enforce other-directed behaviour through coercion. Bentham and the early utilitarians set about rewriting British penal law within that vision. The pain of imprisonment, they held, ought to outweigh the pleasure gained from the crime.

As a more modern, thoroughly secular, take on Spinoza's once-shocking notion that good is simply "that which is certainly useful to us," utilitarianism was a forthright, reductionist approach to morality and moral decision-making. For proponents Bentham and the brilliant father-and-son team James Mill (1773–1836) and John Stuart Mill (1806–1873), the lives of humans, for all their apparent complexity, boil down to the pursuit of pleasure and the avoidance of pain. Based on these psychological assumptions, they concocted a moral philosophy which famously concludes that those actions are *good* which create the greatest balance of pleasure over pain for the greatest number.

The younger Mill's bold foray into human psychology attempted to analyze all human experience in terms of primary "sense atoms" that

---

knowledgeable craftsmen and technicians spawned by nascent industrialism. They called themselves engineers, a group still known for its hard-nosed, positivist worldview. The pioneering sociologist, August Comte (1798–1857) brought similar ultra-rationalist expectations to his field of study (he had for a time served as Saint-Simon's secretary), believing that social intercourse must be governed by invariable natural laws. He called his sociology "social physics." His was an early expression of a soon-to-be universal "physics envy" among social scientists—the desire to place fields of study such as economics, sociology, anthropology, and psychology on the firm, mathematics-based footings of natural law as immutable and predictable as chemistry and hydraulics.

72 W. Stark, ed., *Jeremy Bentham's Economic Writings* (New York: Burr Franklin. Vol. I, 1952. Vols. II, III, 1954), 427–8.

interacted according to fundamental physical laws. Affection, aesthetic feelings, "moral sentiment" and belief were all described by James as compound atomic states which could ultimately be resolved to measurable units of pleasure and pain. Mind, the unobservable enigma, was reduced to behaviour, which could be observed by all. Mind did not cause behaviour—the reverse was true. In this, he agreed with Spinoza: mind was a kind of epiphenomenon—an interesting but ephemeral and ultimately irrelevant side-effect of physical actions, which were determined by physical circumstances. Mind was the motion picture by which we experience our lives, which are determined by immutable physical facts and circumstances.

John Stuart Mill made serious efforts to list various pleasures in ranking order, and even to assign numerical values to them, so that ethical problems might be solved by arithmetic, and social institutions efficiently engineered around algorithms. Inevitably, elements of utilitarianism became embedded in the economic thought that was swirling in the minds of thinkers of the time who often considered themselves both economists and moral philosophers. The elder Mill's *Political Economy* (1848) became an influential classic sometimes favourably compared to Smith's opus.

Because people were inherently "deficient in altruism" and tended to think of work as a disutility ("*Aversion*, not *desire*, is the only emotion which labour, taken by itself, is qualified to produce," Bentham wrote[73]), utilitarians concluded that the only way to advance the cause of civility and prosperity in society was through systematic, structural coercion. This was to be applied humanely, by social institutions engineered to channel "natural" anti-social impulses into communal welfare. Chief among these institutions was the capitalist market economy, which rewarded self-interested behaviour that at the same time produced communal well-being. Age-old English social welfare measures financed by local councils and churches were actively discouraged by the utilitarians as providing an incentive to laziness. The key to dealing rationally with the indolent was to inflict pain upon them in excess of the pleasure they were presumed to derive from their idleness. The poor house and debtor's prisons of Dickensian fame resulted.

Some insight into the role human institutions were to play in the utilitarians' mechanistic world may be had from one of Bentham's cleverest inventions—the Panopticon prison.[74] Pitched to the British government as a money-saving way to incarcerate lawbreakers needing constant surveillance,

---

73 Stark, *Economic Writings*.

74 Jeremy Bentham, *Proposal for a New and Less Expensive Mode of Employing and Reforming Convicts* (London, 1798).

Bentham's design was for a cylindrical building of six stories with a slim central tower in the middle of a large interior courtyard. The doughnut-shaped outer cylindrical structure would be divided into hundreds of individual pie-shaped cells, each with a window on the outside wall, and a door of steel bars facing into the courtyard with its tower.

Seen from above, it had the appearance of a wheel with a hub, but no spokes. The courtyard observation hub was carefully designed (with Venetian blinds, among other features) so that inmates would be unable to see whether it was occupied by guards at any given moment. In this way, prisoners would be isolated from one another, and potentially, at least, under constant surveillance from the watch tower. But, Bentham argued, *actual* constant surveillance would be unnecessary, because prisoners would have to assume they were being watched and behave accordingly. The very design of the building, he said, would condition prisoners to behave as if they were being watched.

Bentham described the Panopticon as "a new mode of obtaining power of mind over mind, in a quantity hitherto without example."[75] A handful of the prisons were built to Bentham's specifications, the best surviving examples of which are on Cuba's Isla de la Juventud, where a group of these buildings, long disused, has been converted to a museum and tourist attraction.

For some, including philosopher Michel Foucault, the Panopticon's model of constant surveillance as an instrument of power delivered via the self-discipline it imposes on the watched, has been fully realized in contemporary culture:

> The panoptic schema, without disappearing as such or losing any of its properties, was destined to spread throughout the social body; its vocation was to become a generalized function. The ultimate result is that we now live in the panoptic machine ... invested by its effects of power, which we bring to ourselves since we are part of its mechanism.[76]

At the time of this writing in, 2023, there are over one billion CCTV surveillance cameras installed worldwide. More than half of them are in China, where there are 374 cameras per thousand people. In Delhi, India there are about 27 surveillance cameras per thousand people. London has

[75] Ibid, The Panopticon Writings, ed. Miran Bozovic (London: Verso, 1995), 29–95.

[76] Michel Foucault, *Discipline and Punish: The Birth of the Prison*, trans. Alan Sheridan (New York, Vintage Books, 1977) p. 207.

about 9.5 cameras per thousand people. Beverly Hills, California, has one CCTV camera for every 17 residents. We can add to this about 17 billion mobile phone devices worldwide, most equipped with cameras.

7. Darwin, Smith, and Kant: Tackling the Alignment Problem

Charles Darwin's watershed theory of evolution, published in *On the Origin of Species* in 1859, combined the by-now-fashionable idea of life as a struggle for existence with earlier notions of evolution—his own grandfather's among them—to produce a mechanism for the development and branching of species that was convincing to scientists. This, in the end, would cause the new science of behaviourism to flourish.

The mechanistic worldview that characterized the Scientific Revolution would henceforth be reinterpreted in terms of interlocking *biological* processes rather than the cause-and-effect meshing of cogs, gears, and cams, as it had been imagined by Descartes, Spinoza, and Hobbes. Motivation for action in humans would be moved from external causes to internal, psychological impulses. But the one system was no less *deterministic* than the other. In both cases, nature operated with a blind, methodical inexorability that was ultimately reducible to mathematical algorithms. There was little room left for free will and therefore little need for metaphysical moral enquiry.

Midway through Queen Victoria's long reign, Darwinian evolution and the utilitarians' radical simplification of human psychology was in this way mechanized to the satisfaction of the biological behaviourists. But there remained a serious unresolved issue. Darwinism and the idea of the "law of the jungle" had resurrected in evolutionary garb a long-standing and very difficult question: how did the collectivist social sense—which led to community and civilization—arise out of the individual's single-minded, Darwinian struggle for survival? As allegedly mechanistic creatures whose behaviour is determined entirely by our physical makeup and environmental circumstances, how did we leap from dog-eat-dog individualism to civilization?

The widely-accepted answer was found in a combination of emergent behaviourism and a modified evolutionary theory. Social behaviour was said to be the result of generations of conditioning by reward and punishment, instilling behaviour that favoured cooperation within groups. Who survives and who succumbs in human evolution was determined not simply by the physical traits of the individual, but also by the "fitness" of the community, its ability to collectively cope with its environment.

That, in turn, was to be measured by the community's ability to control its members, to exercise what was called a "salutary discipline." This amounted to a more scientific expression of Hobbes's philosophical wool-gathering about the beginnings of society in a wary coming together of frightened individuals in search of security and safety.

Remembering that this notion of social beginnings was being promulgated in the age of worldwide European imperialism, it is easy to account for its popularity among social and intellectual elites. Implicit in it was a moral justification for colonialism, among other profitable injustices of the time. In this interpretation of evolutionary theory, Europeans were (self-ascribed) racial and moral superiors over the groups they had subjugated—the evidence of this was provided by the fact of the subjugation. The circularity, and essential emptiness, of this reasoning (indeed, the ability to subjugate was a result of factors other than race and moral fibre) was typical of the behaviourist's attempts to jam the round pegs of complex psychological and sociological phenomena into the square holes of cause-and-effect interactions among perceived "laws" of nature.

Early social scientists of the late eighteenth and early nineteenth centuries, while increasingly interested in research for its own sake, saw their primary role in terms of social engineering, constructing scientifically based, rational institutions for the management of human affairs. These institutions, particularly economic institutions, were designed to complement evolutionary imperatives by reinforcing the kind of "salutary discipline" within communities that enabled them to prosper. Where common sense might envisage social institutions as the bottom-up, organic product of evolving communal conventions and rites—based perhaps on innate moral consciousness and logically beginning with the family—behaviourist thinkers approached them as top-down social *technologies*. These were tools consciously designed for the development of human welfare, even human evolution, through the control and channelling of vicious or unproductive behaviour. It was believed that human imagination, coupled with the unlimited powers of reason, could and should devise technologies that complemented natural law by rationalizing the process of social evolution—correcting for "errors" and inefficiencies. Behaviourist social engineering was Reason compensating for perceived inadequacies in Nature, tweaking the naturally occurring algorithms.

In this era of rapid industrialization with its accompanying dislocation and misery, it is only to be expected that the behaviourist ideology would be recruited as a justifying rationale for the economic policies that were creating such social havoc. The "salutary discipline" that was the evolutionary salvation of Hobbes's nervous savages was re-imagined as the *work ethic*, the application of which sought to counteract two irritating realities about humans—their natural inclination to be content with what they saw as sufficient wealth, and their preference for activities other than salaried labour.

John Stuart Mill had complained that, in the absence of the coercion of rationally organized social institutions, most people will attempt to avoid work beyond what is necessary to support tolerable material comfort. "We look in vain among the working classes in general for the just pride which will choose to give good work for good wages," he said, "for the most part, the sole endeavour is to receive as much and return as little in the shape of service as possible."

To the extent that it existed outside the minds of the privileged classes, this attitude offended against the work ethic as promulgated by Mill and other economists in the early industrial era, according to which one must always give first in order to receive. This was a moral, as well as a practical axiom, and it denied the previously dominant Christian-humanist view that people are of value in themselves, that their worth is not dependent on their productivity. The work ethic asserted further that it was wrong to be satisfied with what one had. As long as there was the possibility of having more (i.e., of satisfying more desires and thus maximizing happiness), one was morally obliged to do the work necessary to get there. This also contradicted not only Christian, but earlier Classical and humanist presumptions, that beyond some level of sufficiency and comfort, additional material wealth was a serious spiritual handicap.

"Work ought to be the normal state of all humans; not-working is dissolute." That was the work ethic's basic presumption, sociologist Zygmunt Bauman notes, and he adds that an important corollary was derived from that idea: "Most people fulfil their duty [to work], and it would be unfair to ask them to share their benefits or profits with others, who could also fulfil their duties but for one reason or another fail to do so." A further, very significant conclusion could be teased out from the logic of the work ethic, which was that "it is only such labour that has value recognized by others—i.e., labour that commands salaries or wages, which can be sold and bought—that has the moral value the work ethic commends."[77] Work, as it was understood in the late eighteenth-century work ethic, amounted to what we would call "the job," a new and for most, unwelcome development in the world. It was not work itself that was endorsed and encouraged (and resisted) but *work on behalf of capital*: i.e., wage labour.

The so-called salutary discipline imposed on workers by the industrial regime—the harsh new regimen of factory toil—was in this way endowed with ethical content. Workers who submitted to it, either willingly, or, more frequently, through coercion, were "bettering" themselves. Those who did not were behaving immorally, and that included the young. In the early 1830s the workday in British textile factories for children aged nine to thirteen was limited by statute to nine hours, and for adolescents from fourteen to eighteen to twelve hours a day. A decade later, further reforms limited the factory workweek for children under eighteen to sixty-nine hours. But to ensure that most of the adult labour pool made the "right" choices, centuries-old Poor Laws in Britain were revised in 1834 on the advice of Benthamite utilitarian theorists and *laissez-faire* liberal economists to make certain that the unemployed were no longer able to live in the modicum of dignity previously afforded by relief

77 Zygmunt Bauman, *Work, Consumerism and the New Poor* (Buckingham: Open University Press, 1998), 5–6.

payments. It was necessary that conditions of life for the unemployed be both physically and emotionally intolerable, and so relief was henceforth provided exclusively in "workhouses" where casual labour was performed in return for basic shelter and a meagre sustenance.

An influential voice in the debate over Poor Laws was economist David Ricardo (1772–1823) whose "iron law of wages" is an excellent example of a tightly-reasoned rationalization of the subsistence wage levels that kept the average worker and his family in a state of precarious near-starvation.

The theory argued that labour was doomed to living on the brink of destitution due to a long chain of mechanical relationships in which capitalists must reap profits if there is to be progress, property owners get rich no matter what, and the worker is doomed to life at the margin. Ricardo wrote, "the natural price of labour is that price which is necessary to enable the labourers, one with another, to subsist and perpetuate their race, without either increase or diminution."

Though there might be periodic fluctuations—like brief periods of plenty—the iron law of wages would remorselessly push workers back down to bare subsistence. Despite this endemic misery, Ricardo concluded with the quintessentially rationalist observation that,

> These then are the laws by which wages are regulated, and by which the happiness of far the greatest part of every community is governed. Like all other contracts, wages should be left to the fair and free competition of the market, and should never be controlled by the interference of the legislature.[78]

Ricardo, as we know him from his biographers, was anything but a misanthrope. The harshness of his theories he saw as realism, a clear-eyed look at the way things have to be. In this, he was deeply influenced by Adam Smith and by his friend and fellow economist Rev. Thomas Malthus, who famously argued that, since population expands faster than agricultural land can be developed (the first growing exponentially, the other arithmetically), humans are doomed to live on the edge of starvation unless stern limits on reproduction are put in place. Malthus

78 David Ricardo, *On the Principles of Political Economy and Taxation*, Ch. 5: "On *Wages*." (1817) (London, Cambridge University Press, 2015).

concluded that such limits are fortuitously imposed by the automatic feedback relationships of the market. Left to itself, in other words, the wretchedness of poverty would limit population growth and thus regulate the labour market through relatively high death rates. It was this sort of fatalistic thinking that prompted the essayist Thomas Carlyle to dub economists "respectable professors of the dismal science."[79]

It's worth noting as an aside that it was Malthus's idea of food scarcity and its effects that inspired Darwin to see the struggle for survival in a world of limited resources as the key to evolutionary theory.[80] The adaptive process had an allegedly virtuous circularity that could be found everywhere in nature, leading to steady improvements in species of all kinds. Darwin himself seems to have adopted an analogy from the competitive dynamic underlying capitalist economics in the *Origin of Species* writing, "all organic beings are striving ... to seize on each place in *the economy of nature*. If any one species does not become modified and improved in a corresponding degree with its competitors it will be exterminated" (emphasis added).

Biologist Richard Lewontin says that, "what Darwin did was take early nineteenth-century *political* economy and expand it to include all of *natural* economy," so that his theory of evolution bore "an uncanny resemblance to the political economic theory of early capitalism." Moreover, its theory of sexual selection was remarkably similar to the gender relations in Victorian society, where "the chief force is competition among males to be more appealing to discriminating females."[81]

---

79 "Neither Charles Kingsley nor Friedrich Engels, neither Blake nor Carlyle, was mistaken in believing that the very image of man had been defiled by some terrible catastrophe. And more impressive even than the outbursts of pain and anger that came from poets and philanthropists was the icy silence with which Malthus and Ricardo passed over the scenes out of which their philosophy of secular perdition was born." Karl Polanyi, *The Great Transformation: The Political and Economic Origins of Our Time* (Boston: Beacon Press, 1944, 2002), 102–3.

80 In the same mechanistic vein, Jean Baptiste Say proposed a Law of Markets (c.1830), which holds that an economy always provides sufficient demand to purchase its own output—regardless of whether workers are paid a fair wage. The obvious implication, once again, was that legislative interference in the market was unnecessary and counterproductive. Say's Law represented consensus opinion in economic theory for more than a century, well into the Great Depression of the 1930s, at which time it was shown conclusively to have no relationship to the real world.

81 Richard Lewontin, *The Doctrine of DNA: Biology as Ideology* (London: Penguin Books, 1993), 10.

In the simplified version of Darwin's theory as it is understood by most people to this day, the underlying rule of "survival of the fittest" leads to constant improvements in species and their ability to survive. This boils down to a tautology, a circular and therefore empty proposition: *viz.* natural selection is the survival of the fittest; the fittest are therefore, by definition, those that have survived.

Like so many of the most influential ideas of early modernism, this take on evolution reflected an eighteenth-century European aristocratic worldview more than any rigorous examination of evidence. Adam Smith writes that participants in a market seek nothing beyond their own personal welfare, the wider economy prospers and grows as a result of their individual actions. Darwin, for his part, proposed that when organisms seeking their own interests compete for scarce resources in their ecosystem, the stronger more adaptable ones survive and thrive with the result that ecosystems grow in complexity and productivity. And as the philosopher Daniel Milo has observed, "Darwinism courses through the ethics of capitalism. The latter's terms—maximization, optimization, competitiveness, innovation, efficiency, cost-benefit trade-offs, rationalization—draw on the authority of Darwinian views of nature."[82]

But it would be a mistake to take from this that either he or Smith found a moral principle such as *greed is good* in operation behind the theories they described, even though both posit self-interest as central to the dynamics they describe. For both men, the foundations of morality lie *outside* these natural processes. Smith writes in his *Theory of Moral Sentiments* (1759) that humanity is guided in its actions not only by a strong will to survive, but also by an instinct he calls "sympathy," although "empathy" and "compassion" better describe what he has in mind. In judging the propriety of their own actions and those of others in the competition for survival, Smith says, "it is not … utility or hurtfulness which is either the first or principal source of our approbation or disapprobation."

The first and principal source of judgement is not any reasoned cost-benefit analysis, but the instinctive empathetic response, a personal, internal evaluation based on an examination of what Smith calls the innate faculty of sympathy, and which we would call our conscience.

82 Milo, *Good Enough*, 2.

This emerges, he says, from our inborn ability to feel the joy and pain of others, and to relate to it.

Darwin wrestled with the morality of the evolutionary processes before arriving at a slightly different, though still naturalistic conclusion, one that reflects the growing popularity of utilitarian philosophy in the intellectual circles of his day. He contrasts two classes of moralists: the utilitarians who believe that what is right is determined by whether and to what degree it promotes happiness; and the realist class which held that, "we have an instinctive moral sense"—an innate moral faculty that operates independently of utilitarian goals and instructs us as to what is right.[83] That hard-wired moral faculty, he believed, evolved out of a long experience with what had proven efficacious for the species in the past.

We should note that neither of these naturalist views provides a satisfactory explanation for the existence and meaning of good. They share in that logical fallacy, tautology: (Smith) how should we define good? That which is useful. How do we define useful? That which is good. Or: (Darwin) how do we know something is good? Because our innate moral judgement says so. Why does our innate moral judgement say so? Because it is good.

Nevertheless, it is safe to conclude that both Smith and Darwin were, in essence, moral realists rather than scientific, moral skeptics as they are often portrayed. Ironically, and despite his undoubtedly good intentions, in describing what he believed was an automated, naturally occurring system for producing moral outcomes, Smith played an outsized role in setting the stage for the eventual marginalizing of authentic moral discourse. In public life, morality was institutionally managed so that actions taken within these institutions were morally neutered, in that each action was merely one in a long chain of causality leading to distant, rational objectives. Bad outcomes were system errors—unintended side-effects that were nobody's fault—rather than ethical failures. Morality was reduced to rules of procedure, which in the economic context were measured according to standards, not of right and wrong, but of efficiency. Morality was, in a word, mechanized.

---

[83] Charles Darwin, "Old and Useless Notes," in *Charles Darwin's Notebooks 1836–1844*, ed. Paul H. Barrett (Ithaca: Cornell University Press, 1987), 30–30v.

8. The Alignment Problem Resolved: Economics as a Moral Science

Adam Smith saw the dynamics of the capitalist market economy as a product of the "laws of nature." In technical language, his theory "naturalized" the market, metaphorically taking it out of human hands and placing it within the purview of natural law—an ordering of nature and humanity's place in it that had been willed by God. Rationalism had thus not entirely eliminated the role of the divine in ordering our economic affairs, but it had demoted God from an active agent in the world to the position of watchmaker or architect, passively presiding over His creation, which for Smith and his followers, included the capitalist market economy. If God had created capitalism, or even just the conditions under which it naturally arose, then capitalism could only be a good thing. Behaviours it encouraged or made necessary would be beyond ethical criticism.

It was the revolutionary notion that good is always already taken care of within the very design of the system that allowed Smith's successors to banish morality from "scientific" economic discourse. As Spinoza might have said, nothing that happens in the market is without necessity. It is thus not the economist's job to raise unanswerable ethical questions about natural market relationships, but to understand their purpose.

This led to the paradoxical situation in which a so-called science of the distribution of scarce goods among competing sources of demand (a formal definition of economics) purports to be value-neutral in its work.

But surely, the lay person might object, normative claims such as justice and equity must obtain. It was a troublesome loose end picked up and resolved by the most influential of the neo-classical economic thinkers, William Stanley Jevons.

Jevons's *General Mathematical Theory of Political Economy* (1862) put economic theory on mathematical footings in a comprehensive way, establishing it as a respectable academic discipline. He saw people as "utility-maximizing" economic agents. "I regard man in reality as essentially selfish," he claimed, "that is as doing everything with a view to gain enjoyment or avoid pain.... This self-interest is certainly the mainspring of all his actions." Borrowing the utilitarian idea of *pleasure* as *value*, he was able to reduce *all* sources of value in classical economics to mathematical formulae, through his ingenious theory of marginal utility.

Marginal utility defines the value of any good or service not by the labour or materials it embodies, but by its utility—by the satisfaction, or benefit, or "pleasure" it brings its consumer. *Marginal* utility is the added amount of pleasure the consumer gets from having an additional unit of a thing. A thirsty person gets a great deal of utility from the first glass of lemonade purchased, but the utility of each successive glass of lemonade diminishes as thirst goes away and satisfaction diminishes. At some point the marginal (additional) utility of additional lemonade falls below the cost (below its monetary value), given that the money being spent could also be spent on some other unsatisfied desire, say, a sandwich.

The way the market operates, Jevons said, is that people, behaving rationally, spread their money around on various purchases in such a way that the added satisfaction (marginal utility) gained from each expenditure is equal. Where there is a disparity, the rational individual directs more of his or her purchasing power toward the most-desired good or service, until the reward from spending equals the total expenditure. Over time, everything balances out and the rational economic agent is content, his or her affordable pleasures having been maximized. That's on the demand side of the supply/demand equation. On the supply side, a business will extend its production up to the point where the cost of producing an additional unit of a commodity or service (i.e., the marginal cost) is just the same as the income received for that unit.

As might be imagined, economists have uncovered endless complexities and paradoxes in the details of Jevons's original theory.

But the truly revolutionary aspect of his formula, still central to modern economics, is that *price and value are to be treated as equivalents*. In other words, the value of anything in an economy is the same as its market-determined price. If a thing has no market price, it has no value. If it does have a price, it has value equivalent to that price. As historian David Noble comments, "the concept of marginal utility [was] a universal solvent that dissolved all other human sources of value."[84] Under Jevons's artful theory, vast areas of moral concern are subsumed, enormously simplifying what had, even in Smith's time, been considered a "moral science," i.e., a branch of moral philosophy.

A century after Jevons and his fellow neo-classical economists, the naturalized approach to economic theory was as robust as ever, in the influential works of F. A. Hayek (1899–1992), a Nobel laureate. As the twentieth century's leading proponent of neo-liberal economics, and, with Milton Friedman (1972–2006), a stalwart of the libertarian-leaning Chicago School, Hayek wrote ecstatically of the market's "transcendent order," to which humanity "owes its very existence." Market dynamics, he said, operate on a plane "which far surpasses the reach of our understanding, wishes, and purposes" and therefore human will ought properly to be subordinated to market forces. "Thy will (i.e., not *mine*) be done on earth as it is in heaven," he wrote of the market's transcendent authority.[85] The phrase, of course, is borrowed from the Lord's Prayer of Christian tradition and is a profession of absolute, willing subjugation of human will to a just and benevolent higher power. The excerpt might well have been extended to include, "give us this day our daily bread ..." and perhaps the rest of the prayer as well.

Heretical or non-conforming viewpoints on the ordering of the world are treated in neo-liberal market capitalism with the utmost seriousness as a threat to the true faith, and therefore to the salvation of humanity. Nations guilty of apostasy are dealt with through sanctions ranging from boycott to invasion (cf. China, Cuba, Venezuela, and Chile).

Since the founding of the World Bank and the International Monetary Fund in 1944, conformity has been organized and regularized through these organizations. The IMF, for example, enforces neo-liberal

---

84 David F. Noble, *Beyond the Promised Land: The Movement and the Myth* (Toronto: Between the Lines, 2006) p. 115.

85 Friedrich Hayek, *The Fatal Conceit* (New York: Routledge, 1988), 6–7, 74, 130–1. Emphasis and brackets in the original. See also his more famous *Road to Serfdom* (1943).

orthodoxy by requiring nations that borrow from it to accept more than one hundred "conditionalities" which ensure compliance with free market conventions and practices. The process of interrogation and renunciation attached to this process is not unlike that employed by the Inquisition in thirteenth-century France.[86]

Neo-liberal ideology has been characterized as a fundamentalist religion that operates in ignorance (or denial) of its own theological nature.[87] Philosopher John McMurtry identifies the particularly close fit between Hayek's free market ideology and standard definitions of theocracy (government in which clerics rule in the name of God). Each system, he reports, imposes "a form of governance in which an infallible authority transcending human agency is represented as the ultimate regulator of daily life, with all understanding, administration, and enforcement of society's rules and laws tolerated solely by compliance with the higher ruler's prescriptions."[88] The market (and note that it is never *a* market or *our* market or *their* market; always *the* market) is tampered with by government at risk of punitive blowback, akin to what might be expected from interfering with a delicately balanced natural ecosystem (or a vengeful deity).

Morality, in much of current economic thought, has thus been swallowed up in patterns of instrumental reason that amount to a simplistic, literalist interpretation of seventeenth-century theories of Hobbes, Spinoza, Leibniz, and their fellow rationalists for whom good is some variation of "that which is certainly useful to us."[89]

With this kind of instrumental reason, priority in economic thought is shifted from ends to means, from the meaning and purpose behind material goals to the most efficient way to attain them. In this context, so far as the market is concerned, there really is no need for moral enquiry because the market automatically produces good (i.e., moral) outcomes. That is, it produces what consumers desire. No need, then, for moral reflection, or even curiosity, when we buy a pair of shoes made in some South Asian sweatshop, or a gallon of gasoline produced from Alberta

---

86 Greg Palast, "The Globalizer Who Came in From the Cold," *The Observer*, October 10, 2001.

87 John McMurtry, "Understanding Market Theology," in *The Invisible Hand and the Common Good*, ed. Bernard Hodgson (New York: Springer, 2004), 152.

88 Ibid, 181.

89 Cf. Ibid, 37.

tar sands or Niger delta offshore crude, or, for that matter, a chicken breast or pork chop carved from an animal grown in inhumane industrial conditions. If it satisfies desires, it's all good.

In modern economic theory, with its utilitarian underpinnings, people are assumed to be "rational economic agents," forever seeking to maximize their own personal gain, because doing so amounts to the satisfaction of desires, which, by definition, produces happiness. Good therefore resides in the fulfilment of desire—*any* desire—because, by definition, desired equals desirable, or good. In other words, according to the algorithm, good is directly related to desire-satisfying consumption, which means that maximizing consumption of a desired thing maximizes good. The American economist and philosopher Clarence Ayres (1891–1972) summed up the moral outlook implicit in neo-liberalism in his classic, *The Theory of Economic Progress* (1981):

> To the question, "What is happiness? Who shall say?" the classical economists seemed to have found a final answer. No one can say; but no one *need* say, since the price system provides an instrument through the subtle operation of which everyone can have a say. Since consumption seems by axiom to be the consummation of all economic effort, and since consumption is actualized in demand, and since demand impacts upon the scarcity of nature to determine the form and direction of every economic undertaking, it seems to follow that *commerce itself expresses in this subtle fashion the aspirations of the race.*"[90]

We should pause here to reflect that reducing the idea of good to "the satisfaction of desires" is as radical a form of moral relativism as can be imagined. It survives because defining good in terms of the satisfaction of individuals' desires for market commodities allows theorists and practitioners of "scientific" economics to sidestep serious consideration of unquantifiable issues of value. Awkward questions are avoided, such as whether the true constituents of one's self-interest are always to be found within the market's material domain, or whether it might be possible, even commonplace, for people to desire what is not in their best interest to have. Or how the interests of others will be affected by my consumption.

[90] Clarence Ayres, *The Theory of Economic Progress* (Chapel Hill, University of North Carolina Press, 1944).

A famous rendering of the issue is found in Saint Augustine, whose transformative theology and philosophy was deeply influential among Protestant dissenters in the Reformation. Freely translated, Augustine says,

> All those are truly fortunate who have what they desire, although not all who have what they desire are therefore fortunate. But they are clearly wretched who either do not have what they desire, or have that which they do not rightly desire. Therefore, he only is a fortunate man, who both has all things which he desires, and desires nothing ill.[91]

It sounds like a riddle, but it makes perfect sense. Good fortune, or happiness, is dependent not just on getting what you want. It depends on both getting what you want and wanting the right things. Wanting the wrong things and getting them is not a recipe for happiness.

What are the right things—the good things—to want? When are desires morally justifiable? Market theory cannot help us with those questions; nevertheless, their significance cannot be denied. In Augustine's formulation, which is so intuitively logical it might be called an axiom, happiness is clearly in some measure dependent on correct moral decision-making. That's especially so when we consider his definition of happiness as the fulfillment of one's potential.

Secondly, philosophers and psychologists agree that it is through the very process of making considered choices among wants and desires—i.e., discovering and prioritizing what is of value to us—that we create an identity, a self.[92] This is how we discover what is truly significant in our lives, and why. In making these choices we construct our core identity. It goes without saying that in our everyday lives those choices will not be based exclusively, or even usually, on the economic formula of cost versus expected utility, on value for money in the satisfaction of wants. That is, they will not be made on a purely instrumental, economic basis, but rather according to a set of criteria that includes moral values and is rooted ultimately in a notion of good that transcends economics.

One more prominent figure on the long trek away from medieval Christian and Renaissance-humanist understandings of value toward

---

91 St. Augustine, *The City of God* c.420 CE (Ch. 5).

92 See, for example, Charles Taylor, *Sources of the Self* (Cambridge: Harvard University Press, 1989).

our own "scientific," instrumentalist approach deserves mention here. The English sociologist Herbert Spencer (1829–1903) was a leading public intellectual during the formative years of early twentieth-century industrial capitalism on both sides of the Atlantic. His ideas, modified to suit changing academic and political fashion, have remained influential as we continue to search for satisfying answers to the question of how to align human values to the design of modern societal institutions.

What began as a scientific hypothesis in Darwin is translated into a cautionary parable by Spencer, one that made him a superstar among the capitalist elites of Britain and, especially, America. In Spencer, the catchphrase "survival of the fittest"—which he coined and only later was adopted by Darwin—becomes a moral imperative, a goal to be actively pursued rather than simply a description of biological processes. He wrote that the final result of Darwinian evolution in an animal species is a stable, completely adapted state "in which evolution can end only in the establishment of the greatest perfection and the most complete happiness."[93] It was clear to him and to his legions of ardent followers in industry's higher echelons that the liberal market system was a powerful accelerator of human evolutionary progress. It followed that self-interest, self-reliance, and competitiveness ought to be encouraged wherever possible.

Spencer was a strong advocate of eugenics, especially as it applied to the often racially motivated elimination of "unfit" members of human society through measures such as forced sterilization. In this he followed the writing of his cousin Sir Francis Galton (1822–1911), a wealthy intellectual prodigy of his time, who devised the term "eugenics" to refer to the agricultural practice of breeding the strongest and most capable of a herd while ensuring that the less able did not reproduce.[94] "Negative eugenics," as it was called, relied heavily on the now-abandoned theories of the French zoologist Jean-Baptiste Lamarck (1744–1829), who believed that physical characteristics acquired by a parent during its lifetime could be inherited by the offspring. The classic example was supposed to be the giraffe, whose long neck was attributed to generations of stretching to reach leaves on the higher boughs of trees.

93 Herbert Spencer, *System of Synthetic Philosophy, Vol. 1 "First Principles"* (1862).

94 "Eu"—Greek: good, well; "genic"—Greek: origin.

In the United States, Lamarckian ideas of heredity were taken up by organizations like the American Eugenics Society, which advocated for racial homogeneity, careful controls on immigration, and the sterilization of the "feebleminded," "degenerate," and "indolent."[95] "High grade" people were urged to reproduce as a social responsibility. The ideas were popularized, appropriately perhaps, at agricultural fairs across the United States in "fitter family" and "better baby" contests. The movement received important support from the American industrialist John Harvey Kellogg (1852–1943), a medical doctor, crusading nutritionist, and businessman. He was the inventor of Kellogg's breakfast cereals including the American staple, Corn Flakes. Kellogg founded the Race Betterment Foundation to promote his ideas and to lobby for their political adoption. He proposed the creation of a national registry that would rate prospective parents according to their racial and other "heritable" characteristics. "Long before the race reaches the state of universal incompetency," he wrote, "the impending danger will be appreciated, the cause sought for and eliminated, and, through eugenics and euthenics [proper nurturing], the mental soundness of the race will be saved."[96]

Applied to late nineteenth and early twentieth-century society, Spencerian ideas developed into a fashionable social philosophy now remembered as "social Darwinism." It proposes that human social progress results from the same self-regulating, competitive processes operating in species evolution, and from this it concludes that suffering, inequity, and injustice in society must be understood and tolerated as essential elements of an evolutionary cleansing process (i.e., survival of the fittest). Measures aimed at easing the plight of the poor and the vulnerable were to be discouraged as delaying the eventual state of "complete happiness" at some undetermined time in the future.

A crucial assumption of social Darwinism in both Spencer and in its adoption by current libertarian economic theory is the rationalist belief that natural systems are highly deterministic: the fate of humanity is in the hands of natural law, and we interfere with its mechanistic, algorithmic unfolding at our own peril. We are truly living in the best of all possible worlds, but we

---

95 In Canada, particularly in the Western provinces, eugenics also flourished in its time. See Angus McLaren, *Our Own Master Race: Eugenics in Canada, 1885–1945* (Toronto: University of Toronto Press, 1990).

96 J. H. Kellogg, "Relation of Public Health to Race Degeneracy," *The American Journal of Public Health* (September 1913): 656.

need to be patient, and avoid the temptation to meddle. Issues of morality, justice, equity, and the like will be taken care of automatically.

The American sociologist Lester Ward (1841–1913) provided a trenchant critique of these remarkably persistent ideas at a time when Spencerism was still in vogue, and it remains as penetrating as ever. Ward noted that a sharp distinction must be drawn between Darwinian species evolution and human social evolution. The first is randomly occurring, essentially purposeless; the second is open to being decisively modified by deliberate human action. Ward observed that the notion of determinism in social evolution does not fit with the fact that humans are creatures of free will, and that in our lives there are not only mechanistic *happenings*, but also purposive, intentional *doings*. In a democracy, people are able to exercise their free will and take deliberate action, and so it makes no sense to abandon society's fate to the alleged automatic systems provided by natural law, especially where these produce injustice.

Ward and other critics of social Darwinism point out that *laissez-faire* liberalism masquerading as natural law results in the survival of the "fittest" only in the crudest sense of the "survival of the big and strong," which suggests that it might more accurately be called the destruction of the weak. But, Ward insisted, "if nature progresses through the destruction of the weak, humanity progresses through the *protection* of the weak."[97] Even if we grant that there is no *telos*, no cosmic purpose at work in evolution (as biological science asserts) there is, Ward insisted, *human* purpose. Whether or not there is transcendent purpose in nature, there can and ought to be in human affairs.

Among the less obvious problems with a natural law approach to economic theory is that it favours leaving in place established social structures. These hierarchies exist, according to this view, at the direction of divine authority, whether or not they are explicitly acknowledged. But the same Renaissance-inspired intellectual ferment that produced market theory as a stand-in for the medieval Christian moral ethos also famously championed Greco-Roman humanist virtues, chief among them the ideal of individual human agency.

An obvious paradox arises: if social structures and hierarchies are to be left untouched, where is the place for individual toil and ambition? Capitalism is above all a system that rewards individual effort, and it does

[97] Lester Ward, "Mind as a Social Factor," *Mind: A Quarterly Review of Philosophy and Sociology*, vol. IX, 1884.

so in a conspicuous way, by bestowing wealth, but where is the space for human agency in such a rigid, deterministic system? One answer would come with the popularizing of a new ideology of meritocracy—a system in which wealth and power accrue to those with talent, education, and a will to work hard.

As a political and economic doctrine, meritocracy fits well with liberal market capitalism, and as a moral system by definition (the Latin word "*meritum*" meaning "due reward") it provides an answer of sorts to nagging questions about the social inequities clearly visible in *laissez-faire* capitalist societies. In a meritocracy, hard work alone is not enough to justify or ensure success. The individual must be endowed with talent and ability and their skills and competencies must be in demand by the market. But given all of this, a person may reach the pinnacles of success and perhaps become a leader. And, surely, rising to those heights of achievement and self-fulfilment can be construed as a moral outcome, as a *good thing* in the sense of fulfilment of natural law.

It is of course a controversial ideology, and the earliest debates about it concerned the meaning of merit itself. Reformation-era teachings equated hard work with prayer, seeing human labour as assisting in the completion of God's earthly creation, but the formal doctrinal relationship seems to have originated with Saint Benedict, founder of the Roman Catholic Benedictine monastic order (c. 500 AD). He coined the motto *laborare et orare*, work and prayer, to describe the dual responsibilities of monks, and in Protestant hands this would often become *laborare est orare,* work *is* prayer, a usage common in the nineteenth century suggesting that hard work generates the merit upon which salvation is contingent. That, at least, was the position of Martin Luther, the great sixteenth-century Christian Protestant reformer. His contemporary, John Calvin, preached the doctrine of a divinely favoured group of individuals who were certain to be saved—the "elect." Salvation could not be earned by earthly works. But in either case, their theologies provided a welcoming environment for evolving capitalism, and a degree of justification for established meritocratic social hierarchies. For the Lutherans, hard work in one's calling could legitimately lead to material wealth; for the Calvinists, ample earthly rewards for effort were seen to be evidence that one was among God's chosen, certain to be saved. Either way, wealth and its accumulation could be seen as morally justified, which was an ideological position of obvious importance to evolving capitalism. Either way, wealth connoted merit, and demanded respect.

But there was an unanticipated difficulty involved in assigning merit to material success, one that was to become clear in the post-World War II experiment with democratic socialism in the United Kingdom. In 1945, the Labour Party overthrew Winston Churchill's Conservatives on a radical platform of free secondary school and adult education, more and better affordable housing, and a single-payer national health service (the much-loved NHS). Informing these and related social welfare measures was a determination to create a more open and equal democracy, where success would be based on merit.

For a while, it looked as though the utopian Labour program was indeed the key to a less class-based, more egalitarian Britain. Wages rose, the work week was shortened for labourers, giving them more leisure time. Housing improved, healthcare was available to all, and demand for higher education soared among those who previously could not have afforded it. A new estate tax on the wealthiest Britons helped to pay for it all. The country seemed on its way to replacing its ancient aristocracy and plutocracy with a meritocracy.

Among the first to see the flaw in this purported meritocracy in Great Britain and other liberal capitalist societies was the brilliant Labour Party researcher who was largely responsible for drafting that inspiring post-war election manifesto, and who coined the term. His name was Michael Young, and he has been called the greatest practical sociologist of his century. The social lives of working classes were his special interest, and his aim as a policymaker was to see that they had ample opportunity to develop their aptitudes and interests and not be held back by a caste system dominated by formal and informal aristocracy.

Although the lives of working-class men and women improved dramatically under Labour's welfare apparatus, the class system, rather than fading away, unexpectedly reorganized itself around meritocratic values. Young explained the dynamic in his 1958 best-selling satire *The Rise of the Meritocracy*. Ostensibly written by a historian looking back from 2023, the book described a society that distributed leadership positions and wealth according to merit, which was defined by the formula: IQ + effort = merit.

In this imagined twenty-first-century society, pluralist democracy would gradually give way to rule by the cleverest, as determined principally by university degrees and other educational credentials taken as measures of intelligence. These well-credentialled men and women would rise to be among the nation's wealthiest, since that is how merit is rewarded in a meritocracy. Those individuals in turn would be parents with the means to lavish attention on their well-connected offspring, giving them every opportunity to develop their talents and intellect through higher education.

In a liberal meritocracy, as theory described it, market outcomes would be brought into line with merit since in a society of equal opportunity, markets automatically reward people with their just desserts. This had been one of Adam Smith's central claims, and the moral justification for laissez-faire economic policy. Assuming equal opportunity, those who reached the top of the heap in such a society would have the satisfaction of knowing that they were there through their own efforts, and that they merited their positions of privilege.

The unfortunate, unavoidable corollary of this selection process, in which neither the luck of birth nor the internal selection processes of institutes of higher education were acknowledged, was that those who languished at the bottom had only themselves to blame: they had been given opportunity after opportunity and failed. They were demonstrably unworthy of success, demonstrably without merit, and thus not worthy of respect.

According to the same formula that allowed society's winners to pat themselves on the back, the losers were, by definition, morally inferior. The term "loser" took on a newly augmented meaning. This of course caused deep, and justified, resentment. As Young himself pointed out in a 2001 editorial criticizing the notoriously meritocratic Labour government of Tony Blair, "it is hard indeed in a society that makes so much of merit to be judged as having none. No underclass has ever been left as morally naked as that."[98]

Young's dystopian novel proved to be prophetic, and nowhere more so than in the United States. Philosopher Michael J. Sandel has summarized the impact of meritocratic ranking in *The Tyranny of Merit*. From the end of World War II to the 1970s, he said, "it was possible for

---

98 Michael Young, "Down with Meritocracy," *The Guardian*, June 29, 2001.

those without a college [university] degree to find good work, support a family, and lead a comfortable middle-class life."

Since then, however, "the earnings difference between college and high school graduates—what economists call the college premium—has doubled. In 1979, college graduates made about 40 percent more than high school graduates; by the 2000s they made 80 percent more." In 2022, it was 84 percent more. Among Americans whose highest academic qualification was a high-school diploma, the unemployment rate hovered around 4.5 percent in 2022; among those with a college degree it was about half that, at 2.2 percent.[99]

Over the decades from the 1970s into the 2000s, globalization led to enormous increases in productivity among wealthy nations, largely through the introduction of robotics and offshoring jobs. Sandel explains that,

> Productivity increased, but workers reaped a smaller and smaller share of what they produced, while executives and shareholders captured a larger share. In the late 1970s, CEOs of major American companies made 30 times more than the average worker; by 2014 they made 300 times more.[100]

And the trend continues: in 2020, American corporate CEOs made 351 times what the typical worker took home.[101]

The resulting resentment at the unfairness of the system and the highly visible inequities it produces has been manifested, not just in the US but throughout the liberal capitalist world, in a populist authoritarianism that is anti-intellectual, anti-expert, and, in that sense, irrational. Spurning the best advice of experts and technocrats, the "meritless" and disaffected often vote against their own best interests, swayed by resentment, and bombarded with targeted, manipulative media messages, electing candidates of dubious qualifications. Those resentments often manifest in conspiracy theories and incoherent rage online, a condition that spills over into real-life violence, as in the widespread displays of populist discontent during the COVID-19 pandemic.

---

99 "TED The Economics Daily," US Bureau of Labour Statistics, July 3, 2023, https://www.bls.gov/opub/ted/.

100 Michael J. Sandel, *The Tyranny of Merit: What's Become of the Common Good?* (New York: Farrar, Straus, & Giroux, 2020), 197.

101 Lawrence Mishel, "CEO pay has skyrocketed 1,322% since 1978," Economic Policy Institute, July 3, 2023, https://www.epi.org/publication/ceo-pay-in-2020/.

The market, it would seem, is failing to do its job. In his landmark survey of sociological findings on happiness in liberal democracies, Yale political scientist Robert E. Lane concluded that, "amidst the satisfaction people feel with their material progress, there is a spirit of unhappiness and depression haunting advanced market democracies throughout the world, a spirit that mocks the idea that markets maximize well-being." The discontent has diverse symptoms that include,

> ... a postwar decline in the United States in people who report themselves as happy, a rising tide in all advanced societies of clinical depression and dysphoria (especially among the young), increasing distrust of each other and of political and other institutions, declining belief that the lot of the average man is getting better, a tragic erosion of family solidarity and community integration together with an apparent decline in warm, intimate relations among friends.[102]

Multiple surveys beginning with the early post-World War II years and continuing to the present show that, beyond the level at which basic needs are met, rising incomes and the things they allow people to buy have little or no statistical correlation with subjective feelings of well-being, or happiness. Other similarly comprehensive studies show that community, companionship, friendship, community esteem, and strong familial bonds, are all strongly related to happiness. The evidence is convincing enough for Lane to conclude that, "the way to increase [subjective well-being] in the United States and probably in all advanced Western societies is to move from an emphasis on money and economic growth toward an emphasis on companionship."[103]

Lane's survey-based research indicates a clear trend away from social intimacy in market societies and toward what he calls Machiavellian

---

[102] Robert E. Lane, *The Loss of Happiness in Market Democracies* (New Haven: Yale University Press, 2000), 3.

[103] Ibid, 7. See also the 2021 Ipsos worldwide survey on happiness, which polled 20,502 adults under seventy-five years of age, finding that, "across the world, people most look to their health and well-being (both physical and mental), their family (partner/spouse and children), and having a sense of purpose as what gives them 'the greatest happiness.' Next on the list come their living conditions, feeling safe and in control, being in nature, having a meaningful job, and having more money." "What Makes People Happiest: Health, Family, and Purpose," Ipsos, July 3, 2023, https://www.ipsos.com/en/global-happiness-survey-march-2022.

relationships. Pressures generated by the market, along with urbanization and industrialization, lead people increasingly to value relationships in terms of their instrumental usefulness, so that we tend to have more and more acquaintances and fewer and fewer close confidants. The same pressures weaken family relationships as well. "Throughout the world," Lane wrote, "the main cost of the imposition of modern market and technological patterns on traditional patterns has been the disruption of interpersonal, especially family, relations."[104] He sees in the mountains of statistical evidence he has amassed a vicious cycle at work: (1) materialism does not lead to life satisfaction or happiness; (2) unhappiness, and especially depression, leads to withdrawal and tends to alienate people; (3) lack of companionship—and companionship is a genuine, if subordinated value for materialists—contributes further to the materialist's unhappiness. Materialists endowed with the qualities that economists assume are the characteristics of winners, tend, in fact, to be losers from the start.[105]

It is worth noting that the evidence Lane and other researchers have compiled indicates that although intimacy through community, friends, and family is crucial to mental health and the avoidance of depression, social media, in lieu of genuine connection, does not contribute to mental well-being. Even among the young, popularity is no replacement for closeness. "Students want confidants, people in whom they can confide, more than friends with whom they can 'hang out,'" writes Lane. And the importance of intimacy increases from youth to middle life. "It might be that market relations increase networks (they are so useful), but it is doubtful that they encourage intimacy (partly because it is so time-consuming)."[106] Emory University ethicist Ira Bedzow explains that,

> ... online communities are replacing familial and communal relationships. These online communities remove the ability for people with different views and varying life stories to find commonality based on a shared life. This is because, unlike actual communities, which are composed of people you encounter as you go about your day, online communities exist by virtue of a shared purpose or function. Friendships in this space, therefore, do not grow for their own sake, and individual members are not valued for

104 Ibid, 117.
105 Ibid, 158.
106 Ibid, 80.

who they are. Rather, their value depends on their loyalty to the group's mission statement.[107]

In 2023, the US Centers for Disease Control's "Youth Risk Behavior Survey" showed that fifty-seven percent of teenaged American girls experience persistent sadness or hopelessness, and nearly a third have seriously considered suicide. Boys are suffering too, but their rates of depression and anxiety are lower. A major cause in both cases appears to be the use of social media, particularly Facebook and Instagram. Studies show a well-defined correlation between the rollout of these platforms and dramatic increases in anxiety and depression among young users worldwide, which can be related to both the nature of the content and decreased time spent sleeping, doing homework, and socializing with family and friends.[108]

Without analyzing the precise microeconomic processes through which mature liberal market capitalism and its associated technologies of information promote radical individualism and impede traditional societal groupings, it is safe to say that the atomized individual stripped of familial and community support is a much easier target for all kinds of organization and control.

Those controlling agencies include the market itself, social and political movements, as well as online media where "positive network effects" are created as individuals are drawn into ideological tribes with the help of AI algorithms. Those network effects in turn make possible the kind of highly targeted advertising—political and commercial—that boosts bottom lines and amplifies political messaging.

Hence, there is a trend in commercial media toward more personalized and fragmented online experiences; away from broadcasting toward podcasting and streaming; away from mass circulation newspapers toward niche online news outlets; away from mass audiences to algorithmic assemblages of individuals sharing demographics, tastes, and political inclinations—the ideal marketing target and revenue source. It is no accident that social media platforms fragment users' attention and impair concentration. It is the distracted

107 Ira Bedzow, "Has Social Media Ruined the Idea of Friendship?" *Forbes*, October 4, 2022.

108 Jonathan Haidt, "After Babel" Substack, February, 22, 2023.

mind that is most susceptible to random information of the kinds supplied by user groups and advertisers. Distraction is in the DNA of these platforms.

The question is whether such developments should be seen as accidental, unintended consequences of the continuing construction of the market system, or something more deliberate. The breakdown of the extended family and its replacement by the much more brittle nuclear family during the twentieth century accompanied burgeoning industrialism, freeing up labour that had previously been tied to family farms, small businesses, and multi-generational households. It further inflated the relative significance of employment and the job in the lives of people, providing a labour force free to up-root and relocate according to the demands of the labour market.

The erosion of family stability has had a markedly greater impact among the middle classes and the poor since about 1960, partly because the affluent minority can afford to purchase the supports necessary for a stable, contented family life, supports that were previously supplied by extended families. The well-off can afford nannies, babysitters, tutors, private schools for their children, and for themselves; vacations, therapy, and the healthy diversions wealth can offer. Writer David Brooks puts it this way:

> If you want to summarize the changes in family structure over the past century, the truest thing to say is this: We've made life freer for individuals and more unstable for families. We've made life better for adults but worse for children. We've moved from big, interconnected, and extended families, which helped protect the most vulnerable people in society from the shocks of life, to smaller, detached nuclear families (a married couple and their children), which give the most privileged people in society room to maximize their talents and expand their options. The shift from bigger and interconnected extended families to smaller and detached nuclear families ultimately led to a familial system that liberates the rich and ravages the working-class and poor.[109]

The cultural historian Jackson Lears offers this critical comment:

> A culture less intent on the individual's responsibility to master destiny might be more capacious, more generous, more gracious. [It] might

[109] David Brooks, "The Nuclear Family Was a Mistake," *The Atlantic*, March 15, 2020.

> encourage fortunate people to imagine their own misfortune and transcend the arrogance of the meritocratic myth—to acknowledge how fitfully and unpredictably people get what they deserve.[110]

In other words, acknowledging the capricious role of luck in human affairs might encourage an appropriate humility among winners, and spare "losers" the mortification of the winners' hubristic contempt.[111]

These trends in liberal meritocracy should be seen as another stage in the continuing project to align human behaviour with the needs of the ideal market economy as abstracted by Smith, Jevons and their fellow classical and neo-classical economic theorists. As we follow the arc of modern economic and technological history from its Enlightenment launchpad, the next supremely important development involves a technological fix to the nagging problem highlighted by Jevons's marginal utility theory.

Equating value with price worked beautifully in the context of market theory, but the troublesome fact was that people do not reliably behave selfishly and aggressively in their market dealings, as the theory requires them to. It was a problem that would be addressed, with spectacular success, by the construction of the modern business corporation, that avatar of the theorist's ideal economic agent. That is the subject of the next chapter.

---

110 Jackson Lears, *Something for Nothing: Luck in America* (New York: Viking, 2003), 34.

111 See the Old Testament's *Ecclesiastes* for the iconic expression of this sensibility: "I returned, and saw under the sun, that the race is not to the swift, nor the battle to the strong, neither yet bread to the wise, nor yet riches to men of understanding, nor yet favour to men of skill; but time and chance happen to them all."

9. The Cyber-Corporation: A Transformative Technology

In the story of the refashioning of *homo sapiens* as *homo economicus*, the story of the emergence of the modern business corporation is of enormous significance, but not widely known. It proceeded little by little, one court case at a time, as liberal market capitalism was fundamentally transforming itself during the first two thirds of the twentieth century.

This metamorphosis of the traditional business corporation was below the radar of all but specialist observers, but it marked the greatest triumph to date for neo-classical economic theory and liberal market capitalism. It represents the most successful and deeply influential experiment in cybernetic machine intelligence undertaken prior to computer science's development of machine learning and large language AI models in the 2020s.

This evolution was, in retrospect, all but inevitable in the context of the *laissez-faire* liberal capitalist market and its system of rewards and punishments for participants both individual and corporate. According to theory, for the market to function optimally its many participants must behave "rationally," that is, in accordance with the canonic assumption of consistent and incorrigible self-interest. But in real life, people often displayed other-directed, altruistic, or in other ways "irrational" behaviour.

Business corporations, on the other hand, reliably behaved the way rational economic agents of economic theory were supposed to.

Their behaviour was accordingly rewarded by the market and by political advocates of free market theory, and today these commercial and industrial behemoths enjoy surprising legal privileges and exert enormous influence over every aspect of our lives.

The term "modern business corporation" as used here has a specific meaning that needs to be defined. First, it does *not* include the small to medium-sized corporations owned and operated by their founders or their successors as family concerns or partnerships which, numerically, are by far the majority in the world of corporate businesses. What the term is intended to signify is the large business corporation that is no longer privately held but listed on stock exchanges and owned by many shareholders, a group that typically includes other corporate institutions such as pension funds, mutual funds, insurance companies and the like. Management positions in the modern business corporation are occupied almost exclusively by university-trained professionals whose primary mandate is to serve the interests of the shareholders. Serving the shareholders is taken to mean one thing: maximizing the monetary return on their investment. This in turn means maximizing corporate profit.

I have called these entities *cyber-corporations* to draw attention to their novelty, and because at their core they are essentially hybrid machine/human entities—cybernetic technologies—that regulate their own operations through feedback from their environment.[112]

Human "management" within them is confined to narrowly prescribed roles and activities that are delineated by the rules, or algorithms, governing the corporate machine's legal and financial existence. Cyber-corporations are intelligent machines, and they play a significant role in governing human society.

The large business corporation of today had its genesis as a straightforward legal resource for the accumulation of capital. As the booming capitalist economy of Europe spun its colonizing web across continents and oceans to Africa, Asia, and the New World in the sixteenth and seventeenth centuries, the potential for realizing vast wealth through trade and commerce was undermined by the enormous risks involved in such far-flung exploratory adventures.

---

112 See Wade Rowland, *Greed, Inc.: Why Corporations Rule Our World* (Toronto: Thomas Allen Publishers, 2005; New York: Arcade Publishers, 2006, 2012).

A solution was found by lawyers, entrepreneurs, and politicians in the creation of the joint-stock corporation, which provided shelter for individual investors from the full impact of financial disaster brought on by, for example, the loss of a ship, or the extermination of a colony or trading outpost by disease or hostile indigenous peoples. A tool developed mainly in Britain, these early "limited liability" (Ltd.) business corporations operated under royal charters, and often served vital foreign policy interests such as colonization.[113] Their structure amounted to a way of socializing risk while privatizing profit, because it frequently fell to outside interests, usually state governments, to deal with the fallout of financial disaster. But it spurred the rapid development of capitalism and its markets by making possible the accumulation and mobilization of large pools of private capital managed by trained professionals.

The corporation as a legal entity has its roots in Roman law, created as a way of securing continuity in the administration of important institutions. By the Middle Ages, royal charters were being granted across Europe to incorporate cities, holy orders, universities, and craft guilds, and increasingly to business enterprises supporting trade and colonization. Each charter conferred a form of immortality on the corporate entity, which was and is separate in law from its human members. Officers of the corporation might come and go, performing their managerial duties until succeeded by others, for as long as the charter remained in force.

The early business corporations, as both reflections and tools of national foreign policy, retained their charters only as long as their activities reflected national goals. Governments saw them as instruments created for special purposes, with a lifespan to be determined by their usefulness in carrying out that purpose.

By the mid-nineteenth century, however, the institution had undergone another transformation. In most jurisdictions, the laws of incorporation no longer required business ventures to fulfill any public purpose in return for the protection and privileges conferred on investors by their corporate charters. As we've seen, it was assumed by this time that public purpose could be safely left in the "invisible" hands of the market mechanism itself. Business corporations had come to be seen not simply as useful vehicles for the undertaking of financially risky but socially beneficial enterprises but also as a good thing in themselves,

113 Examples are the Hudson's Bay Company, the East India Company, the Massachusetts Bay Company, and the Virginia Company.

a helpful adjunct to the rationalist model of the self-governing market mechanism. According to the *laissez-faire* ideology in vogue at the time, the less government interfered with their workings, the more likely it was that social good would result.

The infancy of the business corporation in its present multi-purpose form can be dated to 1811 when the State of New York enacted a law of incorporation that required only a very general description of the type of business being undertaken. The other American states followed suit during the 1840s and 1850s.

In Britain, the Joint Stock Companies Act of 1844 allowed corporations to be created by a simple act of registration with a summary description of the nature of the enterprise.[114] The corporation had transformed itself from a creature of the state—or some monopoly interest in society with clearly defined public benefit—into an all-purpose legal mechanism for facilitating the carrying-on of business within a market economy, its charter no longer subject to any meaningful review.

The nineteenth century in the industrialized world was characterized by mammoth engineering undertakings, including the building of railroads, transcontinental telephone networks and world-girdling telegraph cables, and the opening of vast new regions to farming. Enterprises on this scale called for infusions of manufactured goods such as steel rails, copper wire and glass insulators, farm machinery and grain ships, locomotives and rolling stock, and huge quantities of coal and petroleum fuels. The engineering projects themselves would typically be undertaken by corporations whose stock was widely held, and many of which had been formed with the active encouragement of governments.

This was the case, for example, with the great, continent-spanning railways and telegraph lines of the era. But their capital-goods requirements were still frequently filled by older-style business

---

[114] Summary descriptions were routinely ignored by corporations, despite several court rulings that "object clauses" must be adhered to. In 1966 American courts abandoned this position when the Court of Appeal in "*Bell Houses Limited v City Wall Properties Limited*" approved an object clause giving the Corporation power to: *Carry on any other trade or business whatsoever which can, in the opinion of the board of directors, be advantageously carried on by the company in connection with or as ancillary to any of the above businesses or the general business of the company.*" In 1989 a new Companies Act effectively eliminated the requirement to state the firm's intended sphere of activity in its charter. The power to determine what activities a corporation might legally engage in was transferred from the courts to the corporation.

ventures—partnerships and sole proprietorships. These increasingly obsolescent business entities were stubbornly maintained because they were safe from the public disclosure of financial records that the state demanded of the corporations it chartered. Many of these companies were nevertheless enormous. For example, Andrew Carnegie's Carnegie Steel was a partnership, and several of John D. Rockefeller's Standard Oil affiliates were not incorporated. But the penalty for that privacy, the inability to raise capital by selling shares to the public, became increasingly onerous as economies grew and capital requirements soared.

The trans-Atlantic financial crisis remembered as the Panic of 1873 touched off a long depression that was marked by a frenzy of business mergers in the United States. Undertaken primarily to control overproduction and stabilize markets, these "combinations" or "combines"—monopolies and oligopolies—led to a restructuring of major portions of American industry. The number of partnerships and proprietorships among major business enterprises declined dramatically, and at the same time a great many new and powerful public corporations emerged, their shares trading on stock markets. The era of the robber baron was ending, and the era of the modern business corporation had begun. Between 1899 and 1904, United States Steel, International Harvester, American Can, and twenty-five hundred other corporate mergers changed the face of American business. By 1904, one in ten American workers was employed by a corporation.

As the old business patriarchs died off or were replaced, corporate management was increasingly entrusted to university-trained functionaries who saw all corporations as essentially alike in terms of the skills required to run them efficiently and profitably. A generalized set of professional management techniques stressed not the product or the customer, but the manipulation of corporate capital to maximize the rate of return on shareholder investment. Capital was no longer raised primarily through internal financing but by the sale of shares on the stock market, which meant that ownership, once closely held, was now widely dispersed. These developments had the enormously significant effect of divorcing management from ownership.[115]

---

[115] I mean here ownership in the proprietary sense exemplified by company founders. The late twentieth-century practice of incorporating share ownership in the pay package of senior corporate officers has given these managers a more direct interest in the company's performance. However, the result has often been that corporate managers, increasingly nomadic in their employment, become interested in short-term goals designed to maximize share price (e.g. through layoffs and mergers), rather than

Where the business corporation had once been an extension of the personality of its owner, by the interwar period *it had become the embodiment of pure market theory*, as developed over the previous century and taught in business schools across the industrial world. It had, in other words, undergone another metamorphosis, recast this time into the exemplary "rational economic agent" as imagined by the classical economic theorists, an autonomous creature of pure and unswerving self-interest and with unlimited material desire.[116]

To understand how corporations gained their current personhood status, we need to backtrack a little and recall that the original intent and genius of the corporation had been to provide a means of continuing the life of an institution across generations of human officers. Owners and other principals could come and go, but the corporation itself carried on eternally, without having to reorganize itself with each death or departure. The corporation could be sued, fined, and taxed as an entity, and for these reasons it had always seemed to have a life, a personhood, of its own. But in English jurisprudence of the seventeenth and eighteenth centuries, lawyers acting on behalf of corporations were at pains to insist before the courts that their clients were fictitious or *artificial* persons, creations of the state or political jurisdiction that granted their charter. As artificial persons, they were of course not subject to laws directed at real human people, even though those laws were typically framed in language such as, "no person shall ..." The laws clearly referred to *natural* persons, to human beings.

Toward the end of the nineteenth century, however, and particularly in the United States, corporations and their lawyers changed their age-old tactics as they attempted to minimize regulation by state governments that were responding to a rising chorus of corporate

---

goals that add genuine long-term value to the enterprise. The managers are merely behaving as ethical egoists. It should also be noted that these managers exercise their power over corporate decision-making not through their stock holdings, which seldom amount to a significant percentage of total equity, but through their management positions.

116 The ideology called *managerialism* has its roots in this transition from founder-owners to professional management and the view that business management and an efficient market made democratic government largely redundant. Business managers knew what was best for a country; growth, productivity, efficiency, elimination of waste; all the principles of sound business management. The techniques of sound business management were deemed applicable to any large organization, be it a government department, charitable organization, or university. Managerialism is a sibling to meritocracy.

critics and reformers.[117] They began to press the courts for formal recognition of corporate personhood, and now the plea was that corporations were not artificial, but *natural* persons. The distinction is one of great significance. If corporations are artificial persons, creatures of the state, then the state has the clear right to exercise unlimited control over their activities. If, on the other hand, they are natural persons, like that other race of natural persons—humans—they and their basic rights pre-exist the state. As natural persons, corporations would thus become heirs to primordial "natural rights"—i.e., human rights—intended to protect individuals from government interference beyond what is strictly necessary to maintain civil and social order. They would, in a new sense, be a part of the natural order of things, like the market in which they operated.

In 1886, after years of pressure and lobbying, the remarkable boon of natural personhood was peremptorily granted to American corporations by the US Supreme Court, in the case of *Santa Clara County v the Southern Pacific Railroad*. In this dispute over whether government has a right to regulate transportation fees, the railway framed its case in the legal context provided by the Fourteenth Amendment of the US Constitution, which was written to protect freed slaves from abuse and exploitation. The amendment declares that all state citizens are also American citizens, and (crucially for this case) that no state government shall "deprive any person of life, liberty, or property, without due process of law; nor deny to any person within its jurisdiction the equal protection of the laws." By granting the railroad personhood in this context, the court effectively made it impossible for state governments to regulate railroad tariffs on the movement of agricultural and other products. As natural persons, corporations now had the same rights as human individuals to charge what they liked for their services.

Ignoring some lingering ambiguity on this issue, corporations immediately mounted a concerted legal campaign to gain access to the full panoply of protection offered to human persons under the US Bill of Rights. These vigorous efforts began bearing fruit in a significant way in the mid-twentieth century with a series of Supreme Court decisions that successively granted corporations the same protections as humans under the First, Fourth, Fifth, Sixth, and Seventh Amendments. These

117 Under the American constitution, corporations are creatures of the state governments.

amendments assert the right to free speech; freedom from unreasonable searches and searches without warrants; freedom from double jeopardy; and trial by jury in both criminal and civil cases.[118]

The effect has been to significantly reduce the ability of state and federal governments to regulate, inspect, and exercise control over the operations of corporations. For example, Fourth Amendment protection from regulatory searches without warrants was established in *Marshall v Barlow's Inc.* (1978),[119] in which the US Supreme Court struck down federal Occupational Safety and Health Administration regulations mandating unannounced safety inspections of corporate premises—in this case, the premises of an Idaho electrical and plumbing corporation. Many inspection provisions in federal laws were rendered presumptively invalid by the decision. The court found that corporations enjoy privacy rights equivalent to those of human persons and that commercial buildings should be treated in the same way as private homes under the amendment's protections. A corporation's factory is its castle.

While it is usual to speak of corporations as a capitalist innovation designed to promote the accumulation of capital and its investment in enterprise, an ethical perspective will see this somewhat differently. From an ethical perspective the corporation can be seen to have been designed for the specific purpose of *representing in the market the collective acquisitiveness or self-interest of its shareholders*. Individual shareholders pool their capital, placing it under the control of corporate managers, who are expected as a condition of their employment to maximize the value of those assets and thus the return on investment.

Corporations, as artificial intelligences, are thus self-interested and Scroogelike because they are designed and programmed to be that way. They are simply not expected to be responsible for social welfare because according to the theory under which they are licensed and operate it can be assumed that if they maintain their focus on profit, social good will flow spontaneously, via the automated algorithms of the market. This piece of rationalist ideology was firmly entrenched in US law as early as 1916, in the case of *Dodge v Ford*. As legal scholar and documentarist Joel Bakan tells the story, in 1906, John and Horace Dodge had invested

---

118 A comprehensive archive of key legal precedents related to the evolution of the cyber-corporation can be found at Reclaim Democracy! July 3, 2023, http://reclaimdemocracy.org.

119 *Marshall v Barlow's Inc.* (1962), 369 US 141.

more than $10,000 in Henry Ford's new automobile company and had an exclusive contract to make Ford parts in their Chicago machine shop. Ten years later, the two decided to begin making cars on their own, and they planned to finance the new venture with quarterly dividends from their Ford shares. Their plan hit a stumbling block when Henry Ford, ever the visionary, decided that the profit he was making on his Model T cars was unconscionably high, and that both his company and society at large would stand to gain if he reduced the sticker price. His plan, in effect, was to divert corporate profit to his customers.

The Dodge brothers took him to court, claiming that Ford had no right to give away company profits, however magnanimous his motives. The Michigan Supreme Court agreed. It reinstated the dividend and rebuked Ford for saying in open court that "business is a service, not a bonanza" and that corporations should be run only "incidentally to make money." Ford had erred, the Court said, in forgetting that "a business corporation is organized and carried on primarily for the profit of the stockholders;" it could not be run "for the merely incidental benefit of shareholders and for the primary purpose of benefiting others." As Bakan observes,

> *Dodge v Ford* still stands for the legal principle that managers and directors have a legal duty to put shareholders' interests above all others and no legal authority to serve any other interests—what has become known as "the best interests of the corporation" principle.

Bakan concludes that, "corporate social responsibility is thus illegal—at least when it is genuine."[120]

Corporate philanthropy of course exists, but it must, according to the "best interests" principle, be undertaken in the clear and calculable interest of company shareholders—it must ultimately redound to the bottom line. It must not, in other words, be true altruism. Only the utilitarian brand of pseudo-morality is permitted—only actions undertaken in self-interest which incidentally assist others. Lord Bowen, an English Chancery Court judge with a penchant for metaphor, had expressed a similar view in a precedent-setting 1883 case. "[C]harity has no business to sit at boards of directors *qua* charity," he held. "There is, however, a kind of charitable dealing which is for the interest of those who practice

[120] Joel Bakan, *The Corporation* (Toronto: Viking, 2004), 36–8.

it, and to that extent and in that garb (I admit not a very philanthropic garb) charity may sit at the board, but for no other purpose."[121] The law severely restricts philanthropic activities of corporations, regardless of the views or sentiments of their "managers," and in fact most publicly-traded corporations cautiously limit their philanthropy to about one percent of revenues.

Two of the late twentieth century's most influential economists, Milton Friedman and Theodore Levitt (who both died in 2006), insisted that the role of the corporation ought to be strictly limited to making profit. In a famous article, Friedman asserts,

> I call [social responsibility] a "fundamentally subversive doctrine" in a free society, and say that there is one and only one social responsibility of business to use its resources and engage in activities designed to increase its profits.

Levitt wrote that,

> Welfare and society are not the corporation's business. Its business is making money.... Government's job is not business, and business's job is not government. And unless these functions are resolutely separated in all respects, they are eventually combined in every respect.... Altruism, self-denial, charity ... are vital in certain walks of our life.... But for the most part those virtues are alien to competitive economics.[122]

This moral agnosticism is too often a gateway to immorality or even criminality: cases of corporate malfeasance and resultant damage and are so commonplace that there is no need to catalogue them here.[123] One is entitled to ask, though, if human persons are not exempt from moral responsibility, why are corporate persons so absolved, when they enjoy so many human rights? The divorce of ownership from management functions, the single-minded goal of maximizing profit, the freedom to engage in any field of business, and the ability to challenge government authority from behind the shield of human rights statutes, have all

---

121 Ibid, 38-9.

122 Theodore Leavitt, "The Dangers of Social Responsibility," in *Ethical Theory and Business*, eds. Thomas Beauchamp and Norman Bowie (Chicago: University of Chicago Press, 1979), 138.

123 See, for example, these non-governmental watchdog organizations: https://corporatewatch.org/; http://corpwatch.org.

combined to make the modern business corporation something unique in history. Designed initially as a tool for making money, it has evolved into a highly complex legal entity that is essentially robotic in character, and can accurately be called an artificial intelligence, or cyborg. Its goal remains unchanged—maximizing return on shareholder investment—but its power and influence have been enormously enlarged. And not just its influence on the outside world, where its need for employee mobility contributed to the disruption of the extended family, but perhaps even more profoundly on the work environment itself.

Over the past half-century, sophisticated management techniques and new surveillance technologies have combined to impose internal controls regulating employee behaviour at every level, from the shop floor to the corner C-suites. So effective are these tools that today it seems impossible to avoid the conclusion that the corporate entity *per se* manages its managers, confining them to modes of behaviour that are ultimately defined by the instrumental needs and goals of the corporate person. Those who do not fit this mould are either re-educated to conformity through various forms of coercion, or weeded out.

The situation of humans within the corporate entity is in many ways analogous to the role of modern military personnel, who often operate within an environment defined by the needs and objectives of their weapons systems. As Lawrence Radine explains in *The Taming of the Troops*, "the aircrew of the Apache [attack helicopter] is expected to function reliably *as an extension* of such machines ... or weapons systems generally; [as] adjunct for some limitation the machine has due to its incomplete development."[124] The "machine," in the case of the modern business corporation, is the algorithmic organizational structure, or bureaucracy, that defines its existence. And with each passing year that bureaucracy is more reliant for its efficient functioning on artificial intelligence in its many forms.

The antisocial behaviour of so many of the world's largest corporations in every field from communications and media, to pharmaceuticals, to agribusiness and forestry, to mining, to automobile manufacturing, to finance, and so on, is less baffling if seen in the context of the mature cyber-corporation as a machine-like, self-regulating organism or intelligence. It is designed to

---

[124] Lawrence Radine, *The Taming of the Troops: Social Control in the U.S. Army* (New York: Greenwood, 1977), 89.

maximize the value of the assets under its control, on behalf of its shareholders. External considerations, up to and including human life, are factored into its decision-making only to the extent that they may have an impact on that goal, positive or negative.[125] Ethical interventions by human actors within the machine are limited both by the fear of getting fired, and a kind of cultivated moral myopia. According to psychologist David Luban, there are at least three ways in which corporate structures mute any sense of moral culpability:

> Psychologically, role players in such organizations lack the emotional sense that they are morally responsible for the consequences of organizational behaviour.... Politically, responsibility cannot be located on the organizational chart and thus in some real way no one—*no one*—ever is responsible. Morally, role players have insufficient information to be confident that they are in a position to deliberate effectively because bureaucratic organizations parcel out information along functional lines.[126]

A further analogy is provided by current research into machine learning in artificial intelligence, in which reward-shaping plays an important role. Computer programs coded to include "rewards" for successful computation can lead to explosive progress in intelligence based on self-teaching—machine learning in the conventional terminology of AI.

While the "expert systems" of the late twentieth century required exact inputs and outputs, today's general-purpose AIs need neither. As Henry Kissinger et al. argue in *The Age of AI*:

> These AIs translate texts not by swapping individual words but by identifying and employing idiomatic phrases and patterns.... [S]uch AI is

[125] Cyber-corporations, in their early appearances as actors in emerging, rapidly expanding markets (for example, Bell Telephone at the beginning of the twentieth century, or Google at the century's end), may sometimes seem to have diverse social interests beyond profit. However, as the organization matures along with its market, those experimental interests, which are typically unorthodox, untested approaches to profitability, tend to vanish, along with their champions, in the continuing search for maximum return on investment.

[126] David Luban, *Lawyers and Justice* (New Haven: Princeton University Press, 1989).

> considered dynamic because it evolves in response to changing circumstances and emergent because it can identify solutions that are novel to humans. In machinery, these qualities are revolutionary.[127]

The fear expressed in current AI literature over advanced machine learning that can surpass human capacity and act unpredictably and perhaps dangerously, echoes our real-life experience with intelligent, autonomous, reward-oriented cyber-corporations. Their capacity for destruction is evidenced in our global environmental crisis with its sorcerer's apprentice subtext.

While much attention has been focused on the incubation of AI and machine learning in the form of robots with "general intelligence" and even consciousness, the behind-the-scenes reality of good old-fashioned AI's utility in managing enormous masses of data and finding patterns has in recent decades led to game-changing development of global internet platforms that serve billions of users worldwide.

These corporate entities—Google, Facebook, Twitter, TikTok, Instagram, and WeChat, to name a few—embody unprecedented potential for economic and political influence, given their vast reach and ability to harvest and employ user data.

In relying, by necessity, on automated curation processes, global platforms can "encourage the distribution of certain types of information and the formation of certain types of connections while discouraging others. This dynamic potentially affects social and political outcomes—regardless of the platform operators' intentions."[128] The public release in early 2023 of ChatGPT and a host of other advanced AI technologies for producing texts and images in response to a few prompts from users aroused widespread public alarm among academics, editorialists, and many senior technology developers.

An open letter circulated by a group called the Future of Life Institute and signed by scores of leading tech and AI experts including tech entrepreneur Elon Musk and Apple founder Steve Wozniak called for a moratorium:

---

127 Henry Kissinger, Eric Schmidt, Daniel Huttenlocher, *The Age of AI* (London: John Murray, 2022), 57.

128 Kissinger et al., *The Age of AI*, 112.

> We call on all AI labs to immediately pause for at least six months the training of AI systems more powerful than GPT-4. This pause should be public and verifiable, and include all key actors. If such a pause cannot be enacted quickly, governments should step in and institute a moratorium. AI systems with human-competitive intelligence can pose profound risks to society and humanity, as shown by extensive research and acknowledged by top AI labs.

Musk, in a tweet, commented acerbically, and accurately. "Leading AGI [artificial general intelligence] developers will not heed this warning," he wrote, "but at least it was said." Just days before the time of publication, Musk had already incorporated a firm called xAI to advance the frontiers of artificial intelligence in competition with OpenAI, Google, and Microsoft. When it was officially announced four months later, he told reporters that xAI would build a system that would be safe because it was "maximally curious" about humanity rather than having moral guidelines programmed into it. "From an AI safety standpoint … a maximally curious AI, one that is trying to understand the universe, is I think going to be pro-humanity."[129]

It should be a cause for concern that the risks presented by corporate global platforms and their automated operations is only now being widely discussed. The business corporation has no threshold beyond which risk to human welfare becomes unacceptable, since the only risk it is designed to respond to is risk to profit. Its response to operating in a sphere of activity where risks to human well-being are high, is predictable: it will continue to take risks so long as profitability appears to be secure. It will seek to minimize regulatory oversight wherever possible, because this adds to expenses and forecloses potential avenues of profitability. Of course, the willingness of governments to socialize the potential liability costs of accidents, as they do with nuclear power and with the societal consequences of malicious disinformation, plays into this strategy.

The age-old "precautionary principle" for dealing with risk calls on humans to be prudent about their well-being, and to avoid action where consequences are unknown or unpredictable—that is, where risk

129 Dan Milmo, "Elon Musk launches AI startup and warns of 'Terminator future.'" (*The Guardian*, July 13, 2023)

is high, according to the formula: *risk* = *probability* x *consequence*. But to corporations, prudence is merely a call to scrutiny of risk with respect to the bottom line. A legal strategy for the avoidance of liability lawsuits and regulatory penalties may well be more acceptable to a corporation than a costly engineering policy which would exhaustively analyze human and environmental impacts of products and develop fail-safe design criteria.

The very concept of "risk" in the context of industrially produced societal hazards is early modern, utilitarian, and rationalist. Risk implies that one has done the math to calculate possible harm versus potential benefits connected with some hazard, and that the result has been empirically determined. Depending on that result, a rational agent will sometimes decide to take the risk; on other occasions, to avoid it.

In recent decades, an entire scientific discipline of risk analysis has been spawned by this idea, and the outcome has been the professionalization of judgement about when and whether individuals and groups ought to be willing to accept the presence of industrially produced hazards. The result of this, sadly, has been that action on existing dangers tends to be postponed indefinitely.

Author and political theorist Langdon Winner has summarized the situation this way:

> If we declare ourselves to be identifying, studying, and remedying hazards, our orientation to the problem is clear.... First, we can assume that given adequate evidence, the hazards to health and safety are fairly easily demonstrated. Second, when hazards of this kind are revealed, all reasonable people usually can readily agree on what to do about them.

On the other hand, "if we declare that we are interested in assessing risks, complications ... immediately enter in."[130] These involve myriad scientific considerations of "safe" levels of exposure, precise causal relationships, comparative epidemiological studies, statistical analyses, strategic analyses, and so on. The focus of attention shifts from the hazard to its precise nature and consequences, which are almost invariably matters of intense scientific controversy.

---

[130] Langdon Winner, *The Whale and the Reactor: A Search for Limits in an Age of High Technology* (Chicago: University of Chicago Press, 1986), 143–4. (Emphasis added.)

The question of risk-taking is moved from the moral domain, where ordinary citizens can legitimately claim expertise, to the scientific, where only PhDs need apply. It is now the norms governing the acceptance or rejection of scientific research that are the focus of attention. The result is, to say the least, ironic. As Winner maintains, "faced with uncertainty about what is known concerning a particular risk, prudence becomes not a matter of acting effectively to remedy a suspected source of injury, *but of waiting for better research findings*."[131]

The question can be framed this way: should society be able to say of corporate innovations—like new chemicals, new genetically modified organisms, new gene therapies, new artificial intelligence applications, and global platforms—that they should be considered guilty until proved innocent? Guilty, that is, of presenting a hazard to human or environmental well-being, unless proved innocent of this beyond some agreed-upon standard of evidence? Or, put another way, should society *ever* have to take a risk with technology unless the probable benefit is something beyond increased profit for a corporation?

The presumption of innocence is so deeply ingrained in the Western psyche that we have effectively granted even the corporate person this foundational right under human rights codes. Of course, it makes no sense. Corporations are not human. Corporations are tools.[132]

It can be no accident that the advent of Risk Society in the middle of the twentieth century coincided with the emergence of the fully empowered cyber-corporation as I have described it here. Risk Society is essentially a product of the modern corporation acting out its destiny within the framework of rationalist science and utilitarian morality. Only an entity that had no concept of moral responsibility could radically undermine human health and welfare, and then frustrate attempts by governments to regulate the hazards.

It is corporate, and not human values that are at work in implementing such bio-tech innovations as the "terminator" seed, or human cloning, or bovine growth hormone, or large-scale livestock factory farming,

---

[131] Ibid, 144.

[132] The exception to this is the medical sciences which operate according to the dictum "first, do no harm." New medications of all kinds are, in most places in the world, subject to exhaustive testing and validation before being released to the public. On the other hand, deliberately disruptive new information technologies such as ChatGPT are regularly unleashed on the public with no prior discussion of their possible or probable impacts.

not to mention the industry's attempts to patent genetic sequences and life forms. There are no human values at play in the chemical and pharmaceutical industries' constant, exhaustively documented pressure on state regulatory agencies to be less rigorous in the testing of their products and to relax restrictions on their sale.

Research into the "ethics" of AI is a tiny, underfunded field compared to the industry that has made it necessary. To market products which pose a positive risk, however small, of calamitous damage to human or environmental health is, it seems to me, ethical only under one condition. And that is that the technology in question will, with a high degree of certainty, ameliorate or prevent an even greater calamity. The COVID-19 vaccines fit this criterion. But a great many high-risk products and technologies currently in use and under development do not.

And the negative social impact of generative AI software products like ChatGPT is literally incalculable.

As progress continues with artificial intelligence and machine learning, the potential for catastrophic damage to human interest will only increase. But the fact that this technology is under the control of modern business corporations like Microsoft, Google, and OpenAI should give us pause. As *The Economist* has noted, "the true 'alignment' problem is that AI firms, like polluting factories, are not aligned with the aims of society. They financially benefit from powerful models but do not internalize the costs borne by the world of releasing them prematurely."[133]

As with other problematic technologies in what Winner calls our "risk society," those "externalities" are left to society at large to deal with. It was never intended that corporations become as powerful as they are, and consequently we have no ready-made institutional mechanisms with which to curb their influence and control, and thereby respond to the hazard their operations can present to human well-being.

There is no socialization process for business corporations nor, given their mechanical nature, is one likely to evolve. The only effective linkages between people and corporations are legal ones, and, as they exist today, these are clearly inadequate for the job of ensuring socially responsible corporate behaviour.

We have, in effect, two distinct communities in the heart of the nation—the corporate and the human—and their values are profoundly in conflict. Each has access to the same legal remedies when it feels the

[133] *The Economist,* "How Generative Models Could Go Wrong," April 19, 2023.

other is infringing on its rights. Corporations, however, acting in concert as they do when there is a legal threat, present a formidable, enormously resourceful, adversary before the courts. They employ the best legal counsel available and can afford to extend disputes interminably, exhausting their opponents' enthusiasm and bank accounts. Even national governments are increasingly hesitant to confront this kind of corporate legal might.

When it is combined with equally formidable public relations muscle, and in the US the unlimited political spending rights conferred by the Supreme Court's Citizens United verdict in 2010, political risks of opposing corporate policies and actions can be intimidating.

10. The Tragedy of the Commons

In the tumultuous 1960s and 1970s, the field of economics was profoundly affected by the blossoming field of environmental science, or ecology, which was raising awkward questions about the sustainability of long-established practices of production and consumption. For the first time, in both the pubic sphere and in their private lives, people everywhere in the developed world began to take seriously the possibility that we may be causing irreparable damage to our only habitat, mother Earth.

Paul Ehrlich's *The Population Bomb* (1968), the Club of Rome's *Limits to Growth* (1972), and other books in the same vein did indeed make for gloomy reading. As did a highly influential essay by biologist and ecologist Garrett Hardin, entitled "The Tragedy of the Commons" (1968). Along with historian Lynn White's "The Historic Roots of Our Ecologic Crisis" (1967) and Aldo Leopold's much older book, *A Sand County Almanac* (1949), Hardin's essay, first published in the journal *Science*, is often identified as one of a handful of seminal documents that launched the field of environmental ethics.

Hardin's tract was firmly rooted in the eighteenth-century rationalist tradition. As a disciple of the more deterministic fringes of sociobiology, his concerns about overpopulation led him to hold controversial public opinions on abortion and immigration. On the former, he observed that,

> … a medical abortion, particularly in the early stages, costs only a fraction as much as a medically supported childbirth—not to mention the costs of education and other social services to the child for 18 years. So: when a woman elects to have a child, she is committing the community to something like $100,000 in expenses for the bearing and rearing of that child. Is it wise to extend individual rights that far?[134]

Hardin was well known for his advocacy of "lifeboat ethics," which, like triage in a hospital emergency ward, calculates costs and benefits before determining who should receive life-giving support. On this basis, he favoured tightly restricting immigration to the United States. And he argued that success in reducing infant mortality worldwide would be disastrous for the human species. He and his wife were both members of the Hemlock Society, which advocated legalizing assisted suicide. They took their own lives in their California home in 2003 shortly after celebrating their sixty-second wedding anniversary: she was eighty-two; he was eighty-eight.

These details of Hardin's life illustrate a position nowadays referred to as *scientistic*, denoting an extreme materialism or positivism expressed in an excessive faith in the power of scientific knowledge and techniques. As a noun, it's "*scientism.*"

The "Tragedy of the Commons" proposes a scenario that, on first reading, seems diametrically opposed to the classical economist's creed of the invisible hand of the market turning individual self-interest into communal welfare. For this reason, it caused considerable excitement among 1970s counter-culture environmentalists.

Here was a seemingly irrefutable argument against prevailing capitalist market theory, proof that the consumer society was unsustainable. It also suggested that *laissez-faire* market capitalism did not provide a sure-fire path to the greatest happiness for the greatest number, as conventional theory claimed.

The essay begins with an epigraph in which Hardin quotes himself: "The population problem has no technical solution; it requires a fundamental extension in morality." By the end of the essay, the

134 A 1977 letter to the American Civil Liberties Union quoted in Vaclav Smil, "Garrett James Hardin (Dallas 1915—Santa Barbara 2003)," *American Scientist* 92, no. 1 (January 2004): 8.

reader understands that what he means by "extension of morality" is a replacement of morality with utilitarian-style instrumental reason.

Hardin starts by arguing that human populations will never settle at some optimum, sustainable point as had been predicted in classical and neo-classical economics. "We can make little progress in working toward optimum population size until we explicitly exorcize the spirit of Adam Smith," he wrote. That spirit has "contributed to a dominant tendency of thought that has ever since interfered with positive action based on rational analysis."

If Smith's assumption that private self-interest leads to public welfare via the invisible hand is correct, Hardin continued, "it justifies the continuance of our present policy of *laissez-faire* in reproduction ... if the assumption is not correct, we need to re-examine our individual freedoms to see which ones are defensible."[135]

Hardin wanted that re-examination for reasons he presented in the form of a parable about a common pasture and a group of herders who share it to graze their cattle. He writes,

> Such an arrangement may work reasonably satisfactorily for centuries because tribal wars, poaching, and disease keep the numbers of both man and beast well below the carrying capacity of the land. Finally, however, comes the day of reckoning, that is, the day when the long-desired goal of social stability becomes a reality.

It is at this point, Hardin said, that "the inherent logic of the commons remorselessly generates tragedy." What happens is this: each herder will rationally examine his position vis-à-vis the common pasture and realize that if he adds one more cow to his herd, all of the cattle grazing there will have slightly less to eat, and the land itself will be under a little more stress, but the loss will be more than compensated for him, as an individual, because he will reap the full benefit of the sale of the extra cow. In other words, the positive impact on his position will be something close to +1, while the negative impact he feels will be only a small fraction of -1. Hardin explains,

---

135 Garrett Hardin, "The Tragedy of the Commons," *Science* 162, no. 3859 (December 1968): 1243–1248.

> But this is the conclusion reached by each and every rational herdsman sharing a commons. Therein is the tragedy. Each man is locked into a system that compels him to increase his herd without limit—in a world that is limited. Ruin is the destination toward which all men rush, each pursuing his own best interest in a society that believes in the freedom of the commons. Freedom in a commons will bring ruin to all.

Hardin goes on to say that just such a tragedy is currently brewing worldwide due to the fact that we treat the natural environment as a commons, with the result that polluters continue to dump their wastes there, to the point of environmental disaster in the form of global warming, desertification of the seas, and other catastrophes. He also claims that his parable demonstrates that, without regulation, and according to the same herdsman's logic, people will continue to breed without restraint until the world's maximum sustainable population is exceeded, and population collapse ensues.

Hardin's parable has been justly criticized over the years for presenting human behaviour much as Hobbes did, as determined entirely by innate and unavoidable "natural" responses to the environment. (He is simply wrong, for example, about the dynamics of population growth.) Note the language he uses: we are "locked into" a system that "compels" certain behaviour. Most of us would agree, to the contrary, that humans are capable of behaving sensibly and charitably when faced with a situation such as the one Hardin sketches, and of acting in the interest of the wider community. In fact, this would seem to be, by any objective measurement, our normal mode of behaviour. We humans are prone to altruism, or concern for the other.

Nor does historical evidence support his defeatist outlook. As Jared Diamond notes in his book *Collapse* (2005), Icelandic shepherds of six centuries ago saw that overgrazing was threatening the country's sparse highland pastureland with irreversible erosion.[136] They responded, not as Hardin would have predicted, but by joining together to determine how many sheep the land could support and assigning quotas among themselves.

The fourth-millennium BC Sumerians, on the other hand, did indeed destroy their civilization—the world's first—by overexploiting their arable land. But in their case the danger was not something readily

---

136 Jared Diamond, *Collapse: How Societies Succeed or Fail* (New York: Viking, 2005).

understandable to them. The slow process of salinization of the land caused by too much irrigation was a complex hydrological process that would not be unravelled until the advent of modern science-based agriculture. But where the risk to communal assets is evident and understood, people have historically demonstrated a capacity to suppress short-term avarice and cooperate in the achievement of a longer-term common good.

There is, however, one important actor in our modern market economy that *does* match Hardin's depiction of the incorrigibly rational, implacably self-interested economic agent. That is the cyber-corporation. Wherever the cyber-corporation dominates a commons, the tragedy Hardin depicts is highly likely to be the outcome.

The fact that fish stocks are collapsing in the world's oceans due to overfishing is directly related to the fact that by far the biggest players in the world's fisheries are cyber-corporations. The "soil mining" that results in soil exhaustion and widespread erosion throughout the world is carried on not by individual farmers, but by the mammoth corporations that dominate agribusiness. Mining of mineral deposits in ways that despoil the environment (soon to include the seabeds) is carried out almost exclusively by the cyber-corporations that dominate the mineral extraction industry. Political measures to control climate change by curbing greenhouse gas emissions have been resisted and actively undermined not by individual people, but by the globalized corporations that dominate the fossil energy industry and pool their resources to establish phony "public advocacy" groups.

Where self-employed individuals are directly responsible for damaging the commons, as in the case of farmers or ranchers using slash-and-burn techniques in rain forests, it is invariably the cyber-corporations that create the market conditions that encourage these practices. And it is not individual users of social media platforms who are to blame for their often harmful impacts, it is the corporate business plan of designed distraction and mining of users' data for the purposes of controlling markets and swaying public opinion.

This is not simply a matter of scale. Certainly, the cyber-corporation is typically very large and powerful. But the problem is that, whatever its size and influence, it has no interest in the human interest. As an essentially machine entity, it is not susceptible to feelings of compassion, of shame or pride, of charity or love. Where healthy humans will voluntarily curb their behaviour if they can see that it is harming their neighbour, cyber-corporations alter their behaviour solely according to impact on profit. While they typically present themselves through their public relations as caring, compassionate players in the market, concerned with human welfare at various levels, they do this quite transparently in a bid to maximize profit by cultivating a congenial image.

To put it another way, the cyber-corporation is not interested in virtuous behaviour, only in the *appearance* of virtue, which is reputation. A good reputation is profitable; a bad one is not. For this reason, the cyber-corporation's "virtuous" actions never go unannounced, unpublicized, unadvertised.

This is why cyber-corporations will continue to mine the world's soils and oceans, to dump harmful chemicals into waterways and the atmosphere, to promote the use of dangerous drugs in inappropriate conditions, to exploit adult and child workers, to seek profit from sickness, war, and natural disaster, to expose society to the unintended consequences of inadequately tested information technologies—unless they are faced with strictly enforced regulations that impose penalties greater than the financial gains of their antisocial behaviour.

As a rational economic agent, the cyber-corporation will operate at and beyond the limits of law and regulation (thus maximizing "pleasure") so long as it is profitable to do so. It is not susceptible to moral suasion, except occasionally through boycotts and other forms of consumer revolt, and in this sense, there is no such thing as a "good corporate citizen." Good in this context is mere fiscal prudence.

Corporate social responsibility, a hot topic in business schools everywhere, can be a reality only if it is imposed from outside, through some mechanism that affects profit, in which case compliant behaviour on the part of the cyber-corporation is "responsible" only in the narrow sense of being protective of its own interests. It may be socially responsible in its effect, but not in its intent.

In the wake of the financial crisis of 2008 and the decade of corporate litigation that followed, a retired lawyer named Jamie Gamble, once a partner in a Wall Street law firm that handled the affairs of such major corporations as General Motors, JPMorgan, Chase, Google, and Facebook, wrote an essay that caught the attention of *The New York Times* business section. "Mr. Gamble has had an epiphany since retiring," the *Times* reported, "that is so damning of his former life that it is likely to give his ex-partners a case of agita. He has concluded that corporate executives—the people who hired him and that his firm sought to protect—*are legally obligated to act like sociopaths.*" Gamble wrote,

> The corporate entity is obligated to care only about itself and to define what is good as what makes it more money. Pretty close to a textbook case of antisocial personality disorder. And corporate persons are the most powerful people in our world.

Gamble proposed that corporations should adopt a binding set of ethical standards, approved as by-laws by their boards of directors and addressing relations with key stakeholders like their employees, the communities they serve, the natural environment, and their effects on future generations. Shareholders would then be able to sue should the firm's operations cross the line—just as any board can be sued by shareholders for failing to adhere to the "maximize rule."

Today, he wrote, corporate directors' decisions are evaluated in law according to whether they maximize shareholder value. While there is a loophole called "the business judgement rule," it allows for straying temporarily from that standard only if it can be shown that doing so maximizes shareholder value in the long run. Gamble writes that incorporating ethical rules into corporate by-laws would mean that, "the people charged with acting for the corporation will have to discuss how the corporation should act and will have to account in that discussion for how the corporation's actions affect others. They will have to make a conscience."[137]

What is the likelihood that corporate boards will take Gamble's advice and open themselves to a flood of shareholder lawsuits? Vanishingly small: it's just not in the corporate DNA. Those who have an itch to curb the frequently sociopathic behaviour of the cyber-corporation should therefore focus their interest not on corporate management technique, but on public administration and politics. If the unfettered mechanisms of the market do not deliver communal welfare as promised, then no amount of corporate management expertise will alter that reality. In fact, the more effective and efficient corporate managers become—the better they do their job—the more powerful and therefore potentially dangerous the corporations themselves become. Yes, large corporations

[137] Andrew Ross Sorkin, "Ex-Corporate Lawyer's Idea: Rein in 'Sociopaths' in the Boardroom," *The New York Times*, July 29, 2019.

do create wealth from which not just shareholders but the larger society benefits. But there are other ways to create wealth, and more effective ways to distribute it. That, however, is a different topic.

The tragedy of the commons is real, but it is not a tragedy in the classical form of human beings living out their lives in the grip of ineluctable fate, unable to escape their destinies. It is a robo-tragedy acted out by amoral, machine-like institutions of our own design, set loose upon the world in optimistic ignorance of the eventual consequences.[138] It is a tragedy of blind faith in reason, in technology, in the tools we engineer to manipulate the world around us.

---

138 There were early warnings. Thomas Hobbes and Adam Smith both felt that corporations of their day should be kept on a short leash. US President Abraham Lincoln wrote in 1864, as the Civil War was winding down, that "as a result of the war, corporations have been enthroned and an era of corruption in high places will follow.... I feel at this moment more anxiety for the safety of my country than ever before, even in the midst of war." President Rutherford B. Hayes (elected 1877) warned, "this is a government of the people, by the people, and for the people no longer. It is a government of corporations, by corporations, and for corporations." In 1933, US Supreme Court Justice Louis D. Brandeis referred to corporations as "the Frankenstein monster which States have created by their corporation laws." On the eve of his becoming Chief Justice of Wisconsin's Supreme Court in 1873, Edward G. Ryan warned, "[there] is looming up a new and dark power.... The enterprises of the country are aggregating vast corporate combinations of unexampled capital, boldly marching not for economical conquests only, but for political power.... The question will arise and arise in your day ... which shall rule—wealth or man; which shall lead— money or intellect; who shall fill public stations—educated and patriotic freemen, or the feudal serfs of corporate capital?"

11. Are We Good? The Mystery of Morality Within Us

When Garrett Hardin challenged the long-standing dogma about the capitalist market and its magical invisible hand, he left unexamined classical economics' bedrock assumptions about what motivates people in their public lives. This was a large part of his parable's widespread, if short-lived, celebrity in academic circles and among the commentariat. "The Tragedy of the Commons" was understood to be both ideologically and anthropologically sound, the central supposition being that self-interest, or egoism, is *the* determining feature of human nature.

This prejudice is foundational to all the social sciences and plays an especially important role in economic theory. To quote the classic McGraw Hill undergraduate textbook *Economics*, "Capitalism presumes self-interest as the fundamental modus operandi for the various economic units as they express their free choices. The motive of self-interest gives direction and consistency to what might otherwise be an extremely chaotic economy."

Self-interest as it is understood in economics is not the healthy self-love that is a cornerstone of psychological and spiritual health, because this is unquantifiable. It is rather the material self-interest that exhibits itself in an egoism we call, at its best, acquisitiveness, or at its worst, greed, avarice, lust—those desires that arise out of a preoccupation with the material, and which are commonly called vices, and which foster an ugly competitiveness. And which, thanks to Stanley Jevons's value = price equation, *are* quantifiable.

But what if the assumption—however long-standing and deeply entrenched—is wrong?

There is in fact little or no historical or anthropological evidence that people naturally and habitually act on narrow self-interest in their private or public economic lives. Political scientist C. B. Macpherson and economic historian Karl Polanyi, both respected figures in their fields, agree that, in Polanyi's words, "the behaviour of man both in his primitive state and right through the course of history has been almost the opposite from that implied in this [egoistic] view."[139]

While both writers acknowledge the universality of egoistic behaviour in modern Western capitalist cultures, they both conclude that, "it is only where capitalist relations of production prevail ... that this is the necessary behaviour of all men [Macpherson]," and "the market has been the outcome of a conscious and often violent intervention on the part of government which imposed the market organization on society for non-economic ends. [Polanyi]."[140]

The egoistic behaviour assumed by rationalist thinkers to be a fact of human nature, they argue, is actually behaviour *imposed* on people living in modern market capitalist societies where it is received wisdom that "nice guys finish last." It is behaviour that goes against the grain but is necessary for survival. Liberal capitalist dogma tells us that social institutions were invented as a way to productively channel incorrigibly egoistic behaviour, but the evidence points to habitual self-interest as a mode of behaviour imposed by the social institutions of market capitalism, which were developed to further the interests of prevailing economic powers.

To mistake the realities of egoistic behaviour in market economies for "natural law" is an error Immanuel Kant recognized as early as 1792, in an essay he called "On the Old Saw: That May Be Right in Theory, But It Won't Work in Practice." He wrote,

> One must take people as they are, our politicians tell us, and not as the world's uninformed pedants or good-natured dreamers fancy they ought to be. But *as they are* ought to read *as we have made them* by unjust coercion, by treacherous designs which the government is in a

---

139 Karl Polanyi, *The Great Transformation* (Boston: Beacon Press, 1944, 2001), 258.

140 C. B. Macpherson, *The Rise and Fall of Economic Justice* (Oxford: Oxford University Press, 1985), 89; Polanyi, *The Great Transformation*, 258.

> good position to carry out. In this way, the prophecy of the supposed clever statesman is fulfilled.

Ancient philosophers—Socrates, Plato, and Aristotle in Greece, and their contemporary Mencius, a leading Confucian philosopher in China—have agreed that human nature is either innately good or distinguished by a capacity to know good and an instinctive affinity for it. Plato believed that the human soul partook of a numinous good, which was the fundamental reality and illumination of the universe. Aristotle observed that, "if there is some end of the things we do which we desire for its own sake, clearly this must be the good," and also, bringing this down to earth, "most people would rather give than get affection."[141]

Early Christian philosophy was profoundly influenced by the Greeks, and even Saint Augustine with his notorious emphasis on original sin, conceded that there was an instinct within humans to struggle against the temptations of evil. In Protestant theology of the Enlightenment era, people are capable of distinguishing right from wrong, if only with the intervention of God's grace. Modern Catholicism, since Saint Thomas Aquinas (1225–1274), has taken the position that humans, having been made in God's image, are innately good, and have an in-built sense of right and wrong.[142]

Throughout history, in the major philosophies of East and West there has been a broad and deep consensus that moral consciousness, an innate sense of goodness, precedes moral reasoning and gives it its subject matter. However, economists and rationalist philosophers of the eighteenth and nineteenth centuries, in their determination to free themselves from the intellectual and moral strictures of Christian theology, challenged the ancient idea of an innate moral impulse in people in two ways: by appealing to the experience and observations of their (mainly upper-class) readers; and by disparaging earlier Aristotelian and Christian ideas on the subject. Utilitarian sages, for example, were fond of pointing to the desperate and vice-ridden lives of the Victorian urban poor as evidence that people in their "savage" state were anything but moral creatures. The fact that these well-connected and well-to-do

---

141 Aristotle, *Nicomachean Ethics* (c. 325 B.C.) op. cit.

142 However, because of original sin (Adam and Eve's disobedience in the Garden of Eden) humans have an inherited character flaw that leads them too often to choose wrong over right.

writers themselves, like the rest of their class, were much better behaved was taken as proof of superior discipline resulting from better breeding.

The publication of Charles Darwin's *On the Origin of Species* (1859) and its theory of evolution by natural selection inflated the prestige of liberal market dogma by lending scientific legitimacy to the notion of competitiveness and self-interest as inherited human traits, necessary to progress. It could now be argued that, just as life-or-death competition for food led to the natural selection of the better-adapted individuals in a species, the ruthless competition in market economies weeded out the inefficient economic agents.

But while Darwinian evolution translated into social theory gave us Spencerism, which may still be found in extreme-right political and economic thought and is implicit in today's meritocracy, the central dogma of self-interest as both innate and irresistible is increasingly under siege. In recent decades, a mounting body of evidence has caused even the social sciences to have second thoughts about the plausibility of egoism as the defining characteristic of human behaviour. The science is confirming the opposite, age-old hypothesis.

Recent psychological studies of children confirm what parents know, that there is a strong sense of right and wrong present even in pre-schoolers, and an attraction to the idea and practice of acts of kindness. (The various skills and abilities needed to act on those instincts take longer to develop, as parents learn.)

Vivian Gussin Paley, a noted researcher into childhood development writes of the enormous empathy and respect she had observed in a group of kindergarten kids interacting with a severely disabled child in their midst. "Walking to my hotel," she remembers,

> ... a curious notion enters my mind. When God promises Abraham not to destroy the wicked cities of Sodom and Gomorrah if even ten righteous people can be found, how differently the biblical tale might have ended had Abraham searched in [this kindergarten] classroom.[143]

Field observation and lab experiments with a wide range of non-human animal species have demonstrated that many of them also exhibit genuine altruism in a variety of circumstances. This is behaviour that is

---

[143] Quoted in Susan Neiman, *Moral Clarity* (New York: Harcourt Inc. 2008), 276.

other-directed and for which there is no discoverable payback, immediate or future, either to the actor or its kin-group.[144] Rhesus monkeys will refuse food rather than administer electric shocks to cage-mates; bonobos have been observed helping wounded birds to fly; chimps will hug victims of abuse. From these and many other observations of primates, biologist Frans de Waal has concluded that "we are moral beings to the core."[145]

Examples of altruism among non-primates from elephants to rats and bats, as well, continues to grow both in the academic literature, and more popularly on YouTube, where video evidence proliferates daily.[146] Nevertheless, de Wall notes, while most of his fellow scientists seem perfectly happy to report some animal behaviours as "aggressive," they remain reluctant to characterize other acts as altruistic, or even "sympathetic."

When animals show undeniable tendencies to altruism or tolerance, these terms are typically placed in quotation marks, or given negative labels, as when preferential treatment of kin is called "nepotism," rather than "love of kin." Given that we cannot know the thought processes of other humans, let alone other creatures, this kind of reporting while claiming to conserve objectivity seems rather to indicate bias.

Immanuel Kant offered a helpful thought experiment in support of his contention that the moral impulse is both real and potent. He asked readers of his *Critique of Practical Reason* (1788) to imagine a man walking by one of the many brothels that were a feature of most European cities in his time. The man knows he ought not to go in but is unable to resist the call of lust and pleasure. Now, Kant says, imagine that a gallows has been erected outside the brothel promising certain death to all who enter. Will the man then be able to resist temptation? Of course, he will. His desire for life is far stronger than all other animal passions.

And now imagine that the same man is commanded by his ruler, on pain of hanging, to sign a document falsely accusing an innocent person of an offence punishable by death. The subject of this experiment, we can safely assume, will hesitate, uncertain as to what to do. Nor would any

---

144 Marc D. Hauser, *Moral Minds: The Nature of Right and Wrong* (New York: Harper Perennial, 2006).

145 Frans de Waal, *Good Natured: The Origins of Right and Wrong in Humans and Other Animals* (Cambridge: Mass., Harvard University Press, 1996).

146 See Marc Bekoff and Jessica Pierce, *Wild Justice: The Moral Lives of Animals* (Chicago: University of Chicago Press, 2009).

of the rest of us be sure, given the same circumstances. None of us can be certain that we would do the right thing in the face of death (though history and experience tell us that some of us undoubtedly would). It is in that moment of indecision, Kant says, that we experience our freedom, our ability to triumph over our baser impulses. We also, importantly, demonstrate our knowledge that there is a *right* thing to do.

And it is also in this moment of indecision that we demonstrate the potential for *ideas* to alter the course of events in the physical universe, even against the heaviest of odds. Plato has a simple, and perhaps even more telling experiment: ask yourself, would you rather do evil and be regarded as good, or do good and be thought of as evil? Try it: most of us are at least ambivalent. And it is in our knowing what is right that we demonstrate the existence of moral reality, or, we might say, the existence of *moral fact*.

A book by an American war veteran, Lt. Col. Dave Grossman, deals with an extreme example of innate moral sensibility and its impact in detailing the successes of US military training for Vietnam War troops.[147] In describing the need to overcome soldiers' reluctance to kill, even in self-defence, he notes that while in World War II less than twenty percent of front-line soldiers ever fired their weapons at the enemy, in Vietnam about ninety-five percent had done so. This may be credited, he says, to significant improvement in military training techniques. He notes as well that the post-war mental illnesses suffered by returning Vietnam vets were far worse than those of previous wars. In review of the book, political scientist and philosopher Ned Dobos comments,

> It is difficult to train men (Grossman's data are all from men) to kill efficiently and consistently. The inhibitions to murder seem to be not just culturally generated but also genetic in most people. Breaking those inhibitions demands traumatic psychological and sociological adaptation as anyone who has seen films like Oliver Stone's *Platoon* or Stanley Kubrick's *Full Metal Jacket* will have already guessed. Effectively, recruits are taught to hate, to mistrust everything around them except direct orders, and to exclude moral considerations from consciousness. They are trained as psychopaths.[148]

They are conditioned, in other words, to behave as sub-humans.

---

[147] Dave Grossman, *On Killing: The Psychological Cost of Learning to Kill in War and Society* (Boston: Mass., Black Bay Books, 2003).

[148] Dr. Ned Dobos, "Military Training and Moral Damage," ABC (Australia) Religion and Ethics, July 3, 20223, https://tinyurl.com/5n6d37fe.

But the big question remains: if people have an innate moral sense, where does it come from? Noam Chomsky, one of the contemporary world's most influential scientists and philosophers, was among the first to offer a coherent answer. In a tour de force of combined observation and theory, Chomsky, early in his career, challenged the behaviourist belief that children learn to speak simply by being taught, pointing to evidence that infants are hard-wired with an innate linguistic grammar that makes it possible for them to learn languages. If this were not the case, he was able to demonstrate, they would not be able to become fluent nearly as quickly as they do, if at all.

This finding led Chomsky to speculate that other "grammars" might well be part of human inheritance at birth. "The evidence seems compelling," he argued, "indeed overwhelming, that fundamental aspects of our mental and social life ... are determined as part of our biological endowment, not acquired by learning, still less by training, in the course of our experience."[149]

Next to language, the most probable candidate for such unconscious, innate knowledge seemed to Chomsky to be morality:

> The acquisition of a specific moral and ethical system, wide ranging and often precise in its consequences, cannot simply be the result of "shaping" and "control" by the social environment. As in the case of language, the environment is far too impoverished and indeterminate to provide this system to the child, in its full richness and applicability. Knowing little about the matter, we are compelled to speculate; but it certainly seems reasonable to speculate that the moral and ethical system acquired by the child owes much to some innate human faculty. The environment is relevant, as in the case of language, vision, and so on; thus we can find individual and cultural divergence. But there is surely a common basis, rooted in our nature.[150]

[149] Chomsky's hard-wired grammar theory is not without its detractors. The most popular challenger seems to be "user-based learning," which proposes that children have an innate pattern-recognition ability which, when combined with an innate ability to intuit the intentions of adult speakers they listen to, enables them to learn the basic grammar of any language. To the non-specialist, the difference between the two theoretical approaches seems insubstantial in that the outcomes are the same. The same observation can be applied to innate moral sensibility in children and its sources. In both cases, whatever the theoretical explanation, the result is astonishing.

[150] Noam Chomsky, *Language and the Problems of Knowledge* (Boston: MIT Press, 1988), 161, 152.

The political philosopher and ethical theorist John Rawls arrived at a similar conclusion in puzzling over the roots of morality. He noted, as Chomsky had, the surprising and apparently innate ability we have as young children to recognize and create well-formed sentences, a basic ability which we build on through instruction and experience. And he wrote that moral concepts such as our sense of justice, evident from a very early age, would appear to be constructed on a similar foundation, on an innate, universal *moral* grammar.

As with basic linguistic ability, this grammar is common to all people, but it is expressed differently in different cultures. In the same way as English, Japanese, Arabic, and Urdu are culturally shaped, expressions of a basic linguistic ability among humankind, what we call moral relativism, amounts to more or less superficial cultural variations on a foundational moral grammar that we all share. Rawls insists that "[t]here is no reason to assume that our sense of justice can be adequately characterized by familiar common-sense precepts, or derived from the more obvious learning principles." Our moral capacities, he writes, "go beyond the norms and standards cited in everyday life."[151] As Chomsky writes:

> Why does everyone take for granted that we don't learn to grow arms, but rather, are designed to grow arms? Similarly, we should conclude that in the case of the development of moral systems, there's a biological endowment which in effect requires us to develop a system of moral judgment and a theory of justice, if you like, that in fact has detailed applicability over an enormous range.[152]

If it is the case that our moral behaviour is based on an innate grammar, or disposition, or proclivity, or a specially tailored learning ability, it should be possible to demonstrate this in formal psychological experiments. Remarkably, research into the roots of our abilities to make moral judgments is still in its early stages, but the evidence leans heavily in the direction of Rawls and Chomsky, and few expect that trend to change.[153] Even assuming a satisfyingly positive outcome of those experiments, we will be left with the big question, which

---

151 John Rawls, *A Theory of Justice* (Cambridge: Harvard University Press, 1971), 47.

152 Noam Chomsky, *Language and Problems of Knowledge: The Managua Lectures* (Cambridge: MIT Press 1988).

153 For a comprehensive survey and analysis of this research see Hauser, *Moral Minds*.

science may be unequipped to answer: how can we account for this mysterious ability?

The Enlightenment is sometimes spoken of as an era of disenchantment. This is usually, and justifiably, understood in a positive way, as Reason's triumph in ridding minds of magical thinking, of baseless fears and superstitions. But there is another, less positive, throwing-the-baby-out-with-the-bathwater perspective in which the era's leading thinkers' stubborn repudiation of age-old ways of knowing the world that, while "unscientific," nevertheless can point to profound truths.

Today, such commonplace mysteries as the apparent existence of an innate moral sensibility and its relationship to agency, values, and meaning are accepted as legitimate, mainstream areas of enquiry even though they resist being reduced to the deterministic worlds of biology or chemistry. We are beginning to realize, for example, that the distinction between fact and value is a false and even dangerous dichotomy.

Historians will someday want to look back over the evidence and trace the origins of this welcome development. It may have begun with the startling evidence, uncovered in the mid-twentieth century, that the universe is finite, expanding, and had a beginning at a definite point in time about twenty billion years ago.

This discovery came as an enormous shock to a generation of astronomers, cosmologists, and physicists who had accepted the previous, more comfortable consensus of a steady-state universe that had no beginning and no ending. It forced them to consider questions that their training had not equipped them to answer, such as: if the universe had a beginning, what caused it to begin? Was the universe created out of nothing, *ex nihilo*? Or did something come before?

The trouble is, in the initiating event that science has irreverently dubbed the Big Bang, temperature and pressure were so intense that it is impossible for physical evidence of what might have come before to have survived. The universe was born under conditions in which our laws of physics do not apply. It is a product of circumstances we can never, in principle, know.

Another, even more difficult set of questions raised by the Big Bang involve direction, or *telos*: the universe is evolving from a defined staring point, but in what direction? Toward what end? Is the expanding universe being *pushed* by forces set loose in the Big Bang, or is it being *pulled* by some other (unknowable) agency. If it has a beginning and is evolving, does it also have *meaning*? How might this meaning, or its absence, be influencing humanity?

As astronomer Robert Jastrow writes, "a sound explanation may exist for the explosive birth of our universe, but if it does, science cannot find out what the explanation is. The scientist's pursuit of the past ends in the moment of creation." In other words, science has been confronted with precisely that which rationalists insisted did not exist: a natural occurrence which cannot be explained, even with unlimited time and money. And not just any natural occurrence, but the most fundamental of all. As Jastrow says, "for the scientist who has lived by his faith in the power of reason," the story of the past four hundred years of scientific discovery "ends like a bad dream. He has scaled the mountains of ignorance; he is about to conquer the highest peak; as he pulls himself over the final rock, he is greeted by a band of theologians who have been sitting there for centuries."[154]

Or perhaps a growing wariness of science's claims to exclusive access to reliable knowledge began with mathematician Kurt Gödel's famous incompleteness theorems, which demonstrate with absolute logical certainty that there can *never* be a complete, consistent, mathematical (and therefore, strictly speaking, scientific) description of reality.

Gödel announced in 1931 that any moderately complex system of axioms (i.e., logical/mathematical postulates describing a theory), will generate questions that, though valid and answerable, can be neither proved nor disproved. There will always be true facts about those axioms that cannot be verified by the system.

As an analogy, suppose you had what you believed was a totally complete dictionary: all the words in it must, of course, be defined using other words in that same dictionary. Suppose you then discovered a word that had somehow escaped inclusion in the dictionary—there would be no way to define it, even though it had a definition. There would be no way to know what it meant, even though it had meaning. You could create a new, expanded dictionary to include it, but that dictionary, too, would be open to the same problem—and on and on. With any formal mathematical system, Gödel discovered, there will always and inevitably be loose ends like that.

---

154 Robert Jastrow, *God and the Astronomers* (New York: W.W. Norton, 1978).

The remarkable, unavoidable, takeaway is that theoretical physics, a formal system described in mathematics cannot, in *principle*, provide a complete picture of our world. In other words, Gödel had proved that the basic rationalist conjecture of the Enlightenment—that all knowledge yields to reason—was an error.

There can never be a mathematical (or scientific) description of everything; not all truth is provable, or mathematically describable. What science *can* prove is determined by its own starting assumptions, not by any foundational, cosmological reality. There will always be meaningful knowledge that exists outside of science's purview.

For Gödel, this did not limit fruitful enquiry into the nature of things: it proved, on the contrary, that we live in a world where higher meaning exists. "Our earthly existence, since it in itself has a very doubtful meaning, can only be a means toward the goal of another existence," he wrote to his mother in 1961. "The idea that everything in the world has meaning is, after all, precisely analogous to the principle that everything has a cause, on which the whole of science rests."[155]

Quantum physics pioneer Werner Heisenberg's "uncertainty principle" also casts doubt on the ability of physics to draw a complete picture of the world, but at a more granular level, it demonstrates that it is in principle impossible to know everything there is to know about a sub-atomic quantum particle at any given moment in time. For example, *either* position or momentum of particles such as photons or electrons can be accurately measured and recorded at a given time, but not *both* position and momentum. In all wave-like phenomena—and quanta have features of both wave and particle—the more observers can nail down about position, the less they will know about speed, and vice-versa.

Theoretical physics has had to confront other limits in recent years. Nobel laureate Max Planck, the originator of quantum physics, foresaw this when he wrote in 1932:

> We see in all modern scientific advances that the solution to one problem only unveils the mystery of another.... We must accept this as a hard-and-fast irrefutable fact.... The aim of science is on an incessant struggle toward a goal which can never be reached. Because the goal is of its very nature unattainable....

155 J. W. Dawson, *Logical Dilemmas: The Life and Work of Kurt Gödel* (Boca Raton: A.K. Peters/CRC Press, 1997), 6.

> Science cannot solve the ultimate mystery of nature, and that is because, in the last analysis, we ourselves are part of nature and therefore part of the mystery that we are trying to solve.[156]

Physicists concede that, while quantum theory in its most recent iterations is confirmed by experimental evidence from Europe's hadron collider and other labs, it is also literally "incomprehensible" beyond the esoteric, abstract realm of pure mathematics. Harvard physicist Sheldon Gashow, a Nobel Prize winner for contributions to quantum mechanics, notes that current, advanced ideas such as superstring theory are "far beyond any empirical test." These theories are so far into mathematical abstraction and so far beyond any possible experimental confirmation that, "for the first time since the Dark Ages, we can see how our noble search may end, with faith replacing science once again."[157]

Physicists John Wheeler and David Bohm, among others, have argued that quantum theory clearly indicates that what we call reality cannot be entirely physical, since at its most basic level its existence is predicated on the involvement of a conscious observer. Quanta exist only as statistical probabilities until they are observed, at which time they become either existent or non-existent.[158] The world is, in a literal sense, manufactured by consciousness. Perhaps there is an "implicate, objective order" underlying everything, as Bohm has suggested, a level of reality that is "unknown and cannot be grasped by thought." Bohm has expressed the hope that, in future, science will be "less dependent on mathematics for modelling reality and [will] draw on new sources of metaphor and analogy" such as art.[159]

The lesson seems to be that while what Enlightenment thinkers and their rationalist, scientistic successors created in modern science was immensely fruitful in uncovering the workings of the natural world and in harnessing those discoveries to serve human ends, it was only one way of understanding the world, and, it is now clear, not the only valid

---

156 Max Planck, *Where Is Science Going?* (Woking: Unwin Bros., 1933), 83.

157 Quoted in John Horgan, *The End of Science: Facing the Limits of Knowledge in the Twilight of the Scientific Age* (London: Abacus, 2007), 63.

158 The idea, central to the Standard Model of quantum mechanics, is startlingly similar to Aristotle's notion of a reality that exists *in potentia*, to be brought into existence through interaction with the mind.

159 Horgan, *The End of Science*, 88.

approach to uncovering truth about the nature of things. Ironically, this in itself is no small contribution to our continuing quest for truth.

There seem to be aspects of existence so fundamental, so elemental, that they cannot be described in terms of other features of life and nature, or even in terms of the phenomena they generate. In other words, as the sciences expand their horizons of understanding, at some stage the realities they become aware of may no longer be concrete and specific, but radically basic and transcendent, and therefore opaque to our finite minds, like David Bohm's undiscoverable "implicate order."

Only observation from outside can yield conclusive knowledge about a contained or bounded formal system, and science itself has demonstrated to its own satisfaction that at some level of theoretical enquiry, even in so large a system as the universe, we inevitably run up against definitive boundaries beyond which reason has no power to penetrate. When we reach them, we can only turn inward, calling on intuition, imagination, and the language of metaphor to explain the inexplicable.

Given the truism that our biggest problems are caused not by lack of knowledge, but by believing in falsehood, this new attitude of epistemic humility can only be welcome.

12. Pursuing Post-Human Perfection

Beginning with the Enlightenment era's impetuous determination to free humanity from the yoke of religion and other forms of irrational metaphysical speculation, and from the confining systems of values they produced, Western civilization has evolved through a series of mostly well-intentioned humanistic, scientistic, technological undertakings both "hard" and "soft," social and industrial, that produced unforeseen outcomes of enormous significance. Each of these transformative developments has been seen, both in prospect and retrospect, as *progress*, that ill-defined rationalist concept that appears to be synonymous with nothing more than change over time. They include everything from large-scale utilitarian social engineering—like liberal market capitalism, its attendant consumer culture, and advanced corporate management techniques— through "hard" technologies such as worldwide electronic communication and atomic energy, ultimately onward to current bio-engineering projects aimed at producing AI-enhanced hybrid human beings who will presumably be better equipped to cope with the world as we have left it.

To date, the goals championed by these era-defining developments have been humanistic in that they involved a claim to improving the human condition. But there is an argument to be made that, historically, their effect has been, at least in part, the opposite. What emerges on closer examination is what can only be called a *de*humanizing trend in technology, both social and industrial, that has been gathering steam for at least three hundred years and into which the idea of engineering robotic intelligence fits well. It could be interpreted, in other words, as a long struggle to re-shape human behaviour to conform with the demands of our technologies.

Seen from this perspective, the evolution of strong AI is a natural outcome of an increasingly intimate relationship between humanity and technology, between people and the machines we use to extend and augment our capabilities. Much of this intimacy has been achieved not by aligning technologies to human needs and values, but the reverse. It could be seen as pursuing rationalism to its logical conclusion, laying the groundwork for a hyper-efficient post-humanism.

Western civilization's love affair with machine technology, and the consequent need to better align human behaviour to its needs, really gets underway with the Industrial Revolution of the late eighteenth century, beginning in Britain and spreading through Europe before crossing the Atlantic. Machines powered by steam, and later by internal combustion engines and electricity, increased by orders of magnitude our ability to manipulate the natural environment, extract resources, and transport goods and materials. Scientific discoveries were for the first time systematically transformed into technologies by a new actor on the stage—the professional engineer—who specialized in maximizing the efficient use of resources in production processes. Since a key resource in industrial processes was labour, by the late nineteenth century, engineers were called upon to turn their talents to the design of systems for managing workers and employees.

The engineering interest in the malleability of human nature took two forms, both concerned with the problem of industrial waste and inefficiency via churn in the labour force due to accidents, burn-out, poor morale, and so on. What was known as the "industrial relations" approach aimed at improving the lot of workers to gain their cooperation and loyalty, adjusting industrial conditions to better reflect their needs, and to respond to radical criticisms of capitalism coming from organized labour in the wake of the 1917 Bolshevik Revolution in Russia.

At the other pole was "personnel management" which aimed at moulding, or engineering, society to adapt to industrial conditions using new tools offered by modern psychology and sociology. The two systems shared a perspective on the worker as the object of scientific study and control, imposing on the labour force paradigms of industrial management traditionally applied to non-human resources or factors of production.

Historian David Noble writes, "the scientific management of labour followed directly in the minds of [engineer-managers] from the standardization of materials and machinery. While standardization was the 'elimination of waste in materials' ... scientific management was 'the elimination of waste in people.'"[160] A leading American engineer and educator of the 1920s, Dexter Kimball, observed that, "the extension of the principles of standardization to the human element in production is a most important and growing field of activity."[161]

To achieve this end, leading American manufacturing corporations set up in-house training programs, which were linked in an organization known as the National Association of Corporation Schools, founded in 1913. The NACS and its members would ultimately play an important role in the development of university engineering schools throughout America following World War I. David Noble supplies some representative views from NACS educators,

> "Man-stuff," in the view of Elmo Lewis [of the Burroughs Adding Machine Company], was the "most important thing" with which the companies had to deal. It was the substance "out of which they make their business." E. A. Deeds of the National Cash Register Company agreed; "I am most interested," he said, "in increasing the efficiency of the human machine." In addition to technical proficiency, these educators all stressed the need for training for management. "Electrical engineers," Arthur Williams [of New York Edison, President of NACS] observed, "are from the practical standpoint ... men without peer in running machines, in running plants, but not men trained, necessarily, in running human machines."[162]

In the iconic engineer-manager Frederick W. Taylor's vision, "science would serve to remove the irrational and the emotional dimension of the human element from organizational life, replacing it with formal, rationalistic structures that would ensure maximum efficiency and minimal conflict." In his classic *Shop Management* (1911) he wrote,

> All possible brain work should be removed from the shop and centered in the planning or laying out department, leaving for the foremen and gang bosses work strictly executive in nature. Their duties should be to see that

160 Noble, *America by Design*, 82.

161 Ibid, 82.

162 Ibid, 179.

> the operations planned and directed from the planning room are promptly carried out in the shop.[163]

Erwin Schell, a mechanical engineer by training and an early dean of what would become the Sloan School of Management at MIT, wrote of the professional manager's mission in a 1913 lecture called "The Workmen: Their Impulses and Desires." In it, he discusses how workers' motivations can be reduced to a few basic impulses, and how a skilled manager might use these to their advantage. He writes,

> The executive who, by facilitating promotion … makes marriage a possibility for a young man [thereby dealing with the "Sex Impulse"] stands to receive large dividends in increased loyalty and length of service.… The executive who assigns the new employee a locker, a key, a machine and bench, with name affixed, is bringing instinctive satisfactions to proprietorship ["the Wish to Possess"] which show returns in reduced turnover.… The Desire for Leadership is sometimes called the submissive impulse. I like to think of it, however, as the desire to work under good leadership.[164]

Managers themselves fell victim to the drive to shape individuals to corporate requirements. The successful manager, even today, "dispassionately takes stock of himself, treating himself as an object, as a commodity.… He analyzes his strengths and weaknesses and … then he systematically undertakes a program to reconstruct his image, his publicly avowed attitudes or ideas."[165]

Fordism, named of course for the great industrial innovator, Henry Ford, combined Taylor's scientific management ideas with assembly-line production techniques, giving concrete form to the long-standing technological dream of humans working in perfect harmony with the machinery of production. The ultimate Fordist corporate worker would be a close approximation of an intelligent robot, which would behave perfectly rationally in the context of its mechanical environment, and workplace automation actively fulfils that dream, replacing human

---

163 Quoted in Seymour Melman, *Profits Without Production*, (Philadelphia: University of Pennsylvania Press, 1987), 106.

164 In David F. Noble, *Forces of Production: A Social History of Industrial Automation* (New York: Oxford University Press, 1984).

165 Robert Jackall, *Moral Mazes* (New York: Oxford University Press, 1988), 203–4.

workers with machines. The role of humans in corporate capitalist enterprise was succinctly summarized a generation ago by Noah Kennedy when he said,

> [H]umans fill the roles in productive processes that are uneconomical to mechanize. This should not be a shocking statement, for if any of our jobs could be done at a lower cost by a machine there is no doubt that this would come to pass. Similarly, there is no doubt that each day technology closes in on new intellectual tasks that previously required human intelligence, which is just another way of saying that the task is being rationalized to the point that it can be reduced to formal description and performed by an algorithm. If there is not at this very moment someone formulating a plan for displacing all or part of your labour with machinery, then the sad fact is that you make too little money to make it worthwhile.[166]

With the early twentieth-century popularity of Meyer Bloomfield's "social capitalism" movement, the science of handling workers was extended beyond the factory to their communities. Bloomfield, a pioneering vocational guidance professor at the College of the City of New York, asserted in a 1915 article in the *Annals* of the American Society of Political and Social Science that, "wise business management recognizes the good sense of organizing the *source* of labor supply."[167] This meant instilling desirable physical and mental traits in workers and their children (future workers) at the community level. Corporations established schools and recreation facilities within factories and in adjacent workers' communities. Teaching curricula focused on literacy, fluency in English, and proper work habits. Eventually, the social capitalism idea would motivate corporate complicity, or at least acquiescence, in the construction of the welfare state following World War II.

The late twentieth century saw a swing of the pendulum toward neo-liberalism, Thatcherism, Reaganism, and a new enthusiasm for corporate workplace efficiencies that resulted in waves of "downsizing" and "rightsizing." This era saw a jettisoning of the long-standing social contract between worker and corporate employer that had been implicit

---

166 Noah Kennedy, *The Industrialization of Intelligence* (New York: Unwin Hyman, 1986), 251.

167 Quoted in Stewart Ewan, *Captains of Consciousness: Advertising and the Social Roots of Consumer Culture* (New York: McGraw-Hill, 1976), 18.

in Fordist organizational technique. It was a contract baby boomers can remember their parents having signed on to, the one that brought with it "economic freedom" and the "democracy of (consumer) choice" for workers, in exchange for their voluntary submission to job-for-life loyalty. One kind of freedom was sacrificed at the altar of another.

The successes of scientific management and automation spurred a rapid expansion of industrial output that, as we saw in the history of the corporation, created pressure for corporate mergers and acquisitions on an unprecedented scale in the late nineteenth and early twentieth centuries. These various industrial efficiencies were so effective in increasing the supply of goods and services that they created an urgent need to boost consumption to absorb the excess. Thus, it was during these same years of engineering's first forays into management that the advertising industry initiated its intimate relationship with Sigmund Freud, the behaviourist Ivan Pavlov, and other pioneering psychologists.

The goal was to identify and exploit human frailties and insecurities in the cause of an emerging culture of consumerism, to create and manage people as consumers rather than as producers. By promoting a radical version of Enlightenment liberalism in which the individual's needs and desires are prioritized above all else, and through the very scale of its operations, consumer advertising was able to successfully erode traditional values like patience, thrift, modesty, and moderation, cultivating instead the materialist ethos of envy, acquisitiveness, self-indulgence, and extravagance. This was the long-sought embodiment of the economist's notion of the individual as a perfectly egoistic, rational economic agent.

Marketers pitched "a new logic of living," in which individual liberty was achieved through consumer choice. Buying on credit, formerly known as amassing debt, was pitched as "enforced saving;" a traditional moral hazard was, through the market's sleight of hand, magically transformed into a virtuous practice.[168] In the *Annals of the American Academy of Political and Economic Science* for 1922, consumer advertising was celebrated as, "an instrument of social manipulation" whose purpose is:

---

[168] See, Roland Marchand, *Advertising the American Dream: Making Way for Modernity 1920–1940* (California: University of California Press, 1985) and Stuart Ewen, *Captains of Consciousness: Advertising and the Social Roots of the Consumer Culture* (New York: McGraw-Hill, 1976).

> ... the nullification of the customs of ages ... [to] break down the barriers of individual habits ... [it is] at once the destroyer and the creator in the process of the ever-evolving new; its constructive effort is ... to superimpose new conceptions of individual attainment and community desire.[169]

But modern advertising and the consumer ethic it promoted were about more than the creation and satisfaction of material desires, as Raymond Williams points out in his famous essay "Advertising: The Magic System" (2000).[170]

The consumer ethic, Williams writes, is about the rationalist promise of an enlightened utopian world where progress is never-ending, where tomorrow will always be better than today, where choice is endless, where every emotional and material want is satisfied, where happiness prevails over unhappiness. It is clear, he says, "that we have a cultural pattern in which objects are not enough, but must be validated, if only in fantasy, by association with social and personal meanings which in a different cultural pattern might be more directly available." In short, advertising-supported consumerism is a magical system based on fetish objects, "a highly organized and professional system of magical inducements and satisfactions, functionally very similar to magical systems in simpler societies."

In other kinds of societies, the human needs we address through consumption are filled in other ways, through family and community relations, through religious observances, and service to others.

In the twentieth century, consumer advertising became ubiquitous, in print and outdoor displays, then on radio, then on television, and ultimately online, and not simply as a necessary driver of continuing economic growth. Political advertising with highly condensed messaging aimed at stirring emotional responses, and the parties framing themselves as "brands," would soon become an expensive necessity for successful election campaigns as well.

This made more extensive political fundraising necessary, which in turn led to new relationships of dependency with major donors both corporate and individual. And commercial sponsorship became, in America, an essential source of finance for every aspect of culture, including, crucially, the dissemination of news and information that is a cornerstone of successful democracies. In most of the rest of the world,

169 Ibid.

170 In Raymond Williams, *Culture and Materialism* (New York: Verso, 2005), 170–195.

more circumspect governments recognized the risks involved with dependency on advertising revenue, and the consequent need for public financing of important cultural assets such as broadcasting.

Interest in the manipulation of peoples' emotional, psychological, and even intellectual attributes further broadened throughout the twentieth century and into the next as attention turned to such fields as genetics, reproduction, neurobiology, pharmacology, medical technology, communication technology, and information theory. Technological developments, often unexpected and unprecedented, created needs for rapid and sometimes wrenching social adaptations to accommodate the disruptions, and nowhere was this more dazzling and disorienting than in computer science and information processing.

The development of the new science of cybernetics by the mathematician and philosopher Norbert Weiner and other engineers involved in the war years of the 1940s in such projects as predictively aiming anti-aircraft weapons, suddenly and radically narrowed the conceptual gap between the biological and the mechanical. The two categories were brought together by placing "smart" machines and sentient creatures in the same category—self-organizing, self-sustaining cybernetic systems. (The word is derived from the Greek *kubernetes* meaning "steersman.") It had long been understood that a degree of self-regulation and autonomy in machines can be achieved by feedback loops in which data about the external environment is collected and assimilated by the machine, which then adjusts its operations in response; that, in turn, can cause changes in the environment, completing the loop. A home heating system controlled by a thermostat that reads the room temperature and turns a furnace on or off is the classic example.

In 1948, Claude Shannon's watershed paper "A Mathematical Theory of Communication" provided a powerful adjunct to cybernetics by showing how to quantify, or rationalize, communication of all kinds, both machine and human, by reducing it to algorithms and the manipulation of symbols, and ultimately to the manipulation of "bits"—1's and 0's—in digital computers.[171] It made possible, for example, the digital compact disc recording technology which reduces music performance

[171] See, N. Katherine Hayles, *How We Became Posthuman: Virtual Bodies in Cybernetics, Literature and Informatics* (Chicago: University of Chicago Press, 1999) and George B. Dyson, *Darwin Among the Machines: The Evolution of Global Intelligence* (New York: Perseus Books, 1999).

to bits for efficient storage and reproduces it accurately enough to satisfy most listeners.[172] More significantly, it provided a language with which automated machines could communicate internally, and with one another.

In conceptualizing both mental processes and biology itself as technology, in reducing the biological to the mechanical, the new science of cybernetics was supplying the last pieces for the four-hundred-year-old theoretical model of a rational, mechanistic, deterministic world. A world in which living entities of all kinds are reduced to physical machines governed by algorithms, and therefore completely understandable in rational, mathematical terms.

As the field has advanced since the mid-twentieth century, cybernetics and its prodigal partner artificial intelligence (AI) have made possible, for better or worse, the application of industrial processes to our biological, mental, and social lives. One result is a world in which humans have moved from being participants in self-sufficient communities of producers to acquiring new roles as obedient corporate workers and atomized, compulsive consumers, to finally being a resource mined and processed to supply the data that fuels the new "surveillance economy" run by cybernetic corporate entities.

The phrase was coined by Harvard Business School theorist Shoshana Zuboff, who writes that while twentieth-century Fordist industrialism revolutionized production techniques, the successes of Google, Meta, and other contemporary tech firms have revolutionized extraction techniques. "Industrial capitalism had demanded economies of scale in production in order to achieve high throughput combined with low unit cost," she notes, "in contrast, surveillance capitalism demands economies of scale in the extraction of behavioral surplus."[173]

Behavioural surplus is Zuboff's twenty-first-century analog to Marx's nineteenth-century labour surplus, the source of profit in capitalist markets, the value workers produce for their employers in excess of their wages. It is the information we incidentally and often unknowingly divulge about ourselves and our families when using internet platforms including search engines and social media, data that is

---

172 To achieve complete accuracy CD recording would need to involve an infinite sampling rate which is of course impossible. Analog vinyl recording is therefore the choice of many audiophiles.

173 Shoshana Zuboff, *The Age of Surveillance Capitalism: The Fight for a Human Future at the New Frontier of Power* (New York: Public Affairs, 2019), 86.

assiduously collected and used to profile our wants, needs, and desires. This information is sold to advertisers and others who are willing to pay money for our online attention to their tailored, targeted messages. The process amounts to a transformative advance in efficiency over the twentieth-century commercial media's hit-or-miss approach to selling self-selecting TV or radio audiences in bulk to advertisers. And it is making tech firms enormously wealthy and powerful while eroding the very idea of personal privacy.

13. The End Game

The search for artificial intelligence was confidently undertaken in the aftermath of World War II on the assumption that the electronic computer could be trained to mimic the human brain. Confidently, because as Thomas Hobbes had asserted and the founders of modernism agreed, "reasoning is but reckoning."

Reckoning was something even the wartime vacuum-tube computers did exceedingly well, breaking "unbreakable" German ciphers in time to turn the tide of combat. The standard criterion proposed for machine intelligence at that time and well into the future was the so-called "Turing test,"[174] in which a human evaluator communicates via text with a pair of examinees closeted in another room, one of them human, the other a computer. If after asking a series of questions of each, the evaluator is unable to tell which of his communicants is a computer and which a person, the computer is deemed to be intelligent. In retrospect, it seems a remarkably naive standard. It repeats Francis Bacon's seventeenth-century fallacy that scientific descriptions that "save all the appearances" are equivalent to definitive explanations.

In other words, a map and the territory it describes are essentially identical, or in this case, an exact imitation is qualitatively the same

[174] Proposed by Alan Turing, mathematician, logician, and inventor of the general-purpose electronic computer. A classic is provided by John Searle in his "Chinese room" thought experiment which appeared in "Minds, Brains, and Programs," published in *Behavioral and Brain Sciences* in 1980.

as the original. In the Turing test, which Alan Turing himself dubbed the "imitation game" in 1950, a computer that can convincingly fake human intelligence is deemed to be intelligent itself. Three quarters of a century onward, anyone with a laptop computer can download a version of ChatGPT that will do exactly that.

It seems self-evident, though, that machine intelligence can never be more than *machine* intelligence. It cannot duplicate, or "surpass," human intelligence for the simple reason that human intelligence is biologically embodied. That is, it is an evolutionary feature of a particular kind of sentient, living creature in which it exists not just in neuronal processes in the brain but is distributed throughout the body. What we call "muscle memory" is a familiar expression of embodiment, and when memory acts, it is often impossible to separate its intellectual, emotional, chemical, and muscular components. Human intelligence is deeply influenced by the surrounding environment, as it is experienced through elaborate sensory systems peculiar to the species. Moreover, human intelligence is a product of culture, historic and current, to such an extent that it makes little sense to speak of the individual human intellect without acknowledging that connection.

As physicist and philosopher David Bohm writes, human thought is, in an important sense, collective: "most of our thought in its general form is not individual. It originates in the whole culture and pervades us.... This deep structure of thought, which is the source, the constant source—timeless—is always there."[175] Moral knowledge, which is implicit in humans (and perhaps other species as well) would appear to belong in this "deep structure" category. Related to this is what Michael Polanyi calls "tacit knowledge"—skills, ideas, and intuitions that humans possess, knowingly or otherwise, but cannot easily express in words.[176] It is knowledge that comes with lived experience. It is why "book learning" is no substitute for "hands-on" experience, and why we apprentice with experts, understanding that to extract such knowledge from another person often requires close contact over time, as in a mentorship. It is what enables us to derive meaning from language.

---

175 David Bohm, *On Dialogue* (London: Routledge, 1996).

176 Michael Polanyi, *Knowing and Being* (Oxford: Routledge and Kegan Paul, 1966), 133. Polanyi, a scientist and philosopher whose achievements are so wide-ranging as to resist categorization, is usually described in biographies as a polymath.

Riding a bicycle, driving a car, or playing a musical instrument, or building fine cabinetry, or diagnosing obscure illnesses, or writing good poetry, or developing elegant scientific hypotheses are all examples from daily life where tacit knowledge is essential. For Polanyi, the accumulation of tacit knowledge is a process common to all living things and has been going on since life emerged on the planet. It has shaped the evolution of species individually and collectively. In humans, it is a large part of what accounts for selfhood, the individual, and unique "me." Polanyi believed that all living organisms possess some degree of tacit knowledge of the world around them, enabling them to survive. A great deal of what we know as humans consists of this kind of knowledge, much of it all but impossible to put into words. As Polanyi says, "we know more than we can tell."[177]

The depth and complexity of the deep structure of knowledge—of tacit knowledge—plus the fact that we are in most cases unable to express it in explicit terms, means that it is all but impossible to translate it into the language of computers. Nor will it be available to computers through access to even the largest internet-based databases. Given the still-unknown potential of machine learning in computers, it is impossible to say whether a form of machine tacit knowledge might emerge, but it cannot in principle duplicate tacit human knowledge.

The idea of thought and knowledge as embodied can seem counter-intuitive because it turns on its head an important aspect of rationalist culture, and current conventional wisdom. Descartes's mind-body dualism, with mind being a separate, non-material substance—the "ghost in the machine" as the behaviourist Gilbert Ryle scoffed—is replaced by the idea that thought emerges organically as the physical body interacts with its environment. [178] To conceptually separate mind and body, as Descartes did, is to misunderstand the essence of thought as inescapably the product of a material process.

This is not to say that mind itself ought to be placed in the category of "material" but to acknowledge, as current quantum physics strongly

---

177 Polanyi, *Knowing and Being*, 133. In neurological terms tacit knowledge may be associated with what early brain-scan experimenters saw as random "noise" in the "resting" brain. See Johannes Bruder, *Cognitive Code: Post-Anthropocentric Intelligence and the Infrastructural Brain* (Kingston: McGill-Queen's University Press, 2019).

178 Gilbert Ryle, *The Concept of Mind* (New York: Routledge 1949, 2009).

suggests, that the material world is "not just mechanical."[179] There is more to matter than meets the eye. Mind (or consciousness) and matter seem to be "entangled" in a way that is analogous to the fact/value relationship discussed earlier.

In January of 1999, the last year of the old millennium, three books were published that set the agenda for animated public conversations about what it means to be human in the age of robots, cyborgs, and "machine learning."[180] All three predicted a new century in which humanity's flesh-and-blood-borne consciousness would be superseded by self-teaching AI running on silicon chips. The machine intelligences would eventually take charge, like Hobbes's Leviathan, simply by weight of superior intellect. The first and most obvious question this prediction raises is, why would we want to create such a "post-human" future? To what end? In all three books, the implied answer reaches back to Francis Bacon and the Enlightenment ethos in which technological advance is, by definition, *progress* in some normative sense, preordained and morally and inherently desirable.

Beyond the technological change = progress tautology. The direct answer given by computer scientist Hans Moravec and like-minded futurists is that we have no choice. The age of the intelligent machine is *inevitably* the next stage in evolution of the human species, in which we are replaced by post-human entities. Once evolution has created human intelligence through natural selection, the argument goes, it is only a matter of time before that intelligence creates smart technology, which creates super-intelligence within super-computers, and teaches itself how to learn independently. The logical next step is for the super-intelligence to supplant (or enslave) humanity, just as humans had earlier used their superior intelligence to gain dominance over other, inferior species. This is scientific determinism taken to an absurd, even obscene, extreme. But it is also a straight line in reasoning from the initial assumptions of the rational scientistic worldview born in the sixteenth-century Enlightenment and nurtured through succeeding centuries by economic interests and their allies in politics and academia (see Chapters 5–8).

---

179 Bohm, *On Dialogue*, 95.

180 Ray Kurzweil, *The Age of Spiritual Machines: When Computers Exceed Human Intelligence* (New York: Penguin, 2000); Hans Moravec, *Robot: Mere Machine to Transcendent Mind* (Oxford: Oxford University Press, 2000); Neil Gershenfeld, *When Things Start to Think* (New York: Henry Holt & Co., 2014).

These days, YouTube videos excitedly show robots navigating their environment and doing human-like chores, but it is a mistake to think that a machine capable of duplicating a human's activities in the material world would necessarily be of equivalent intelligence to its human counterpart. It is an even bigger mistake to assume that such a machine, no matter how adept, is conscious. Even if we leave aside the very human issue of motivation, what drives us to act, we can simply assert that a person's external behaviour is far from being a complete representation of his or her inner consciousness or inner, subjective being—an insight missed by B. F. Skinner and other behaviourist psychologists of the early twentieth century.

Humans are able to pretend, fake pain, mimic the behaviour of others, and make deliberate errors. There is much more to human consciousness than is displayed in external human behaviour. The same cannot be said of robot behaviour. Or can it? One can imagine a computer scientist proudly saying of her latest AI creation that it "clearly exhibits consciousness." The problem then becomes, how to prove it. We have no clear understanding of *human* consciousness, but what we do know after centuries of scientific enquiry suggests strongly that it is a manifestation of the subject's embeddedness in a biological body which in turn is the product of millions of years of evolution amid the myriad challenges presented by the Earth's environment. The idea of "programming in" consciousness of this kind seems frankly absurd, as does the notion of machine learning manufacturing it.

Post-humanist futurism simply takes for granted that the human mind is essentially a very powerful computing machine. Information theory lends support to this idea by reducing communication, including human thought processes, to the mere manipulation of symbols and the uncovering of patterns—processes at which computers are demonstrably very good. The fact that computers may at some time in the near future exceed the capacity of the human brain in the number of computations carried out per second does not mean, however, that such a computer will be a more powerful mind. The human mind does manipulate symbols, but it also does much more.

Human minds incorporate (or exhibit) consciousness, which remains mysterious, both scientifically and philosophically. Some computer scientists have proposed that consciousness is an emergent property of the complex system that is the human body and brain, and that therefore the spontaneous emergence of consciousness in machines is only a matter of time, a matter of their reaching the necessary level of complexity in their computational abilities.[181] But a careful reading of emergence theory shows that whatever property emerges from a system, it is certain to share the essential characteristics of that system. It cannot be otherwise in a material world. In which case, machine "consciousness," should it happen, would be utterly different from that which produces human thought.

Human minds provide us with subjective, real-world experiences that are central to our lives as human beings—experiences like introspection, the excitement of discovery, the awe of mystery, the love of others, the joy of being alive. Human minds engage in the creation of the self, the unique individual capable of self-reflection and self-recognition, self-doubt and self-assurance, self-love and self-hatred, desire and intention, and so on. These are processes of such complexity and mystery that, again, it seems preposterous to suppose that any computer program could be designed to mimic them. Even if it could, to replicate, or mimic, is not to reproduce. The reflexive self is surely something that can only evolve naturally, organically, and within a social setting.

The philosopher and computer scientist Joseph Weizenbaum writes in his classic *Computer Power and Human Reason* that,

> No other organism, and certainly no computer, can be made to confront genuine human problems in human terms. And, since the domain of human intelligence is, except for a small set of formal problems, determined by man's humanity, every other intelligence, however great, must necessarily be alien to the human domain.

It follows, he warns, that even though computer-based "expert systems" can, in principle, be used, for example, in clinical diagnoses and judicial judgments, "since we do not have any ways of making computers wise, we ought not to give computers tasks that demand wisdom."[182] This conclusion, it seems clear, can safely be extended to include the

181 See, for example, Ramon Guevara, Diego M. Mateos, and José Luis Pérez Velasquez, "Consciousness as an Emergent Phenomenon: A Tale of Different Levels of Description," *Entropy* (Basil) vol. 22(9) p. 921: Michael Brooks, "Emergence: The Mysterious Concept That Holds The Key To Consciousness," *New Scientist*, May 10, 2023

182 Joseph Weizenbaum, *Computer Power and Human Reason: From Judgment to Calculation* (New Orleans: Pelican, 1976), 227.

hypothetical next step in technology, called artificial general intelligence (AGI) which can train itself autonomously and perform any intellectual task humans or other conscious creatures are capable of doing.

Any machine, electric, electronic, or mechanical, if it is to do what it is designed to do, (if it "works") must operate within a set of design parameters or rules of operation, which are established by its builder. Even AI programs that are designed to learn from their experience (that is, to revise their own programming on the go) do so only within the framework of their original design parameters. Therefore, any "consciousness" exhibited by such a machine, "would be simply an accompaniment to mechanical operations" beyond its agency.[183] What a computer scientist might proclaim to be consciousness—*eureka!*—can be nothing more than his or her (human) interpretation of that spurious accompaniment. The consciousness, in this case, would reside in the interpreter.

This much, at least, seemed secure opinion before the late 2022–2023 releases of Microsoft-funded ChatGPT, Google's PaLM, and related machine learning, large language programs that can draw on the immense trove of data, of human knowledge and information, stored in text, audio, and video on the internet.[184]

The explosive expansion of their abilities in so many fields has raised legitimate questions about whether, in fact, a semblance of sentience or consciousness might one day be realizable. The best answer, based on the information presented above, remains "no" as pertaining to an authentic self-consciousness, and "perhaps" in the case of a convincing, synthetic imitation.

Think of AI as the endpoint of a centuries-long trajectory beginning with the Enlightenment's conceptual mechanization of mental processes, biology, and the world in general. If we accept modernity's notion that progress for our species is to be defined as increasing technical ingenuity and sophistication, it is logical that the culmination should be the actual, not merely figurative, mechanization of humanity: naturally evolved

---

183 Michael Polanyi, *Personal Knowledge* (Chicago: Chicago University Press, 1964), 336.

184 It is beyond the scope of this book to discuss in detail the technologies of AI including neural networks, large language models, machine learning, transformers, and deep learning. It is worth noting, though, that the latest iterations of programs like ChatGPT defy even their creators' abilities to explain in detail their inner workings.

human intelligence creates machine intelligence which then creates super-intelligent machines.

We can leave that, for the moment, to the world of sci-fi. Although not without noting that a 2021 survey by the polling company AI Impacts reported that five percent of AI experts surveyed said they expected the outcome of advanced AI on humanity was likely to be "very bad" and another ten percent said "bad." (Ten percent responded with "extremely good" and another twenty percent with "good.")[185]

In the interim, the widely-proclaimed promise of AGI (artificial general intelligence) in the twenty-first century is that it will eradicate disease and inherited disability, it will eliminate the drudgery attached to too much of our work, leaving only fun and satisfying parts of jobs; it will dramatically improve the efficiency and quality of policy formation and decision-making in business and government; it will ensure the continuance of the species in the face of existential threats like climate change or an asteroid collision, by making possible the colonization of Mars; it will strengthen the ability of individuals to independently pursue their own desires and needs; it will provide companionship for the lonely and information of all kinds to satisfy curiosity and educational needs.

In other words, it will create, at last, the utopia promised so long ago by the Enlightenment savants as a realistic alternative to the ethically good life so vainly sought by moral philosophers of old and the major religions. It will accomplish this, in a word, by making us smarter, more technically adept.

We need to ask, though, whether a lack of technological smarts is really what underlies our failure to bring climate change under control, to alleviate suffering caused by social and economic inequity, to provide justice for the disadvantaged and marginalized among us, to provide an environment in which all can flourish? Do we really have an urgent need for what AI is offering in the new generative large language models? To choose just one example, the solutions to climate change are already well-known and are being adopted around the world, albeit too slowly, and only reluctantly. As the environmentalist Naomi Klein writes, that's because:

> ... doing what the climate crisis demands of us would strand trillions of dollars of fossil fuel assets, while challenging the consumption-based growth model at the heart of our interconnected economies. The climate crisis is not, in fact, a mystery or a riddle we haven't yet solved due to insufficiently robust

[185] https://blog.aiimpacts.org/p/how-bad-a-future-do-ml-researchers

> data sets. We know what it would take, but it's not a quick fix—it's a paradigm shift. Waiting for machines to spit out a more palatable and/or profitable answer is not a cure for this crisis, it's one more symptom of it.[186]

Given experience with the initial rush to market with AI, it would seem certain that the old patterns of corporate profit-seeking which are justified by a reliance on "risk assessment" and the magic of the market to ensure ethical outcomes are determining AI's future. OpenAI, the developers of ChatGPT, was founded as a non-profit counterweight to the power and influence of the corporate behemoths of Big Tech. But in 2019, it reorganized as a for-profit corporation and shortly thereafter received a $10 billion investment from Microsoft. At the time of this writing, OpenAI's market value was about $30 billion. Its products are central to Microsoft's attempt to unseat Google from its long-standing perch as leader in the ultra-profitable field of internet search.

Geoffrey Hinton, whose work has been foundational to developing the large language-neural network models that power the new generation of AI products left his senior position at Google in 2023 so that he could speak openly about the risks presented by the technology. He told *The New York Times* that in the information environment fostered by AI applications, nobody "will know what is true anymore." Oxford University's Institute for Ethics in AI senior research associate Elizabeth Renieris worries that, "advancements in AI will magnify the scale of automated decision-making that is biased, discriminatory, exclusionary or otherwise unfair while also being inscrutable and incontestable." She notes that AI tools that are trained on human-created content, text, art, and music, and are then able to imitate them, "free ride" on the "whole of human experience to date," and their corporate creators "have effectively transferred tremendous wealth and power from the public sphere to a small handful of private entities."[187]

In her *Guardian* essay Naomi Klein put it this way,

> We are witnessing the wealthiest companies in history (Microsoft, Apple, Google, Meta, Amazon...) unilaterally seizing the sum total of human

---

186 Naomi Klein, "AI Machines Aren't 'Hallucinating.' But Their Makers Are," *The Guardian,* May 8, 2023.

187 Chris Vallance, "Artificial Intelligence Could Lead to Extinction, Experts Warn," *BBC,* June 30, 2023.

knowledge that exists in digital, scrapable form and willing it off inside proprietary products, many of which will take direct aim at the humans whose lifetime of labor trained the machines without giving permission or consent.

She noted that the industry leaders like former Google CEO Eric Schmidt have for years been conducting a lobbying campaign,

> ... telling both parties in Washington that if they aren't free to barrel ahead with generative AI, unburdened by serious regulation, then western powers will be left in the dust by China. Last year [2022], the top tech companies spent a record of $470 million to lobby Washington—more than the oil and gas sector—and that sum, Bloomberg News notes, is on top of the billions spent on their wide array of trade groups, non-profits and thinktanks.

Given corporate realities, the impact of flooding the market with AI technologies that can successfully carry out the work of people in a host of industries from transportation, to art and design, to journalism, to accounting, to healthcare, and so on will not be that these unemployed people, Klein states, "are suddenly freed to become philosophers and artists. It means that those people will find themselves staring into the abyss."

Let's recapitulate. Throughout history, both religion and philosophy have understood morality to be related to—indeed, a manifestation of—a universal good that exists as a feature of the world, either through unknown causes related to the origins of the universe, or due to the nature of, or will of, a divine Creator. Both religion and philosophy—and some scientists, too, though with some reservations—have concluded that humankind partakes of this good. It does so either as having been created "in God's image," or by virtue of being an evolutionary product of all the basic components of the universe. The result in both cases is that humans (and other sentient creatures to varying degrees) share what moral realists call an innate moral sensibility, an impulse to be *for* the other.

It is on the baseline reality of this moral sense, demonstrable in history, the laboratory, and in day-to-day experience, that moral realism builds its case for the existence of moral fact, or universally valid and truthful moral precepts, and adds the word "critical" to its name. Critical moral realism argues that the existence of this body of moral knowledge presents an obligation to enquire, explore, and discuss points of convergence and divergence with others. This process leads to the creation and reinforcing of consensus, which, if it survives enough challenges over time, can be taken to be fact—though never, given human imperfections, definitively and for all time. The best we will ever be able to say is that we are as certain of (this fact) as we are of anything we know.

Why should it matter whether our culture has a clear understanding of the sources of morality? Because we know in great detail the origins and character of the problems the world faces, thanks to science, and we also have some good ideas, again thanks to science, about how to ameliorate them. The failure to act on that knowledge—to take decisive action against global warming for example—arises not so much out of indifference, as a kind of moral disorientation. The loudest and most bellicose of the political voices in current media are those that deny the validity of moral standards or ethical rules, dismissing them as "political correctness," or power-tripping elitist sanctimony. Thus, anyone claiming moral motivations—a desire to do the right thing—is by definition a self-serving hypocrite, because no such "right thing" can exist. In the face of this, we find it difficult, if not impossible, to make moral judgements, to say "that is just plain wrong," or "this is certainly the right thing to do." The standard rejection of moral argument as "just a subjective opinion" ultimately expressing one's self-interest can be difficult to counter.

In the absence of such confidence, we are prey to the failings of that very self-interest, and of cynicism. The forces of unexamined rationalism, the amoral cyber-corporations, the mercenary lawyers, the cynical politicians, the opportunistic religious leaders, the nefarious propagandists with their AI bots, all have their agendas, talking points, and rationalizations, and are hard to confront in the absence of any unifying vision of a better world.

Modern information technology enjoys powerful positive network effects and a potent self-reinforcing circularity as it advances at breakneck speed toward what its developers see as its manifest destiny in AGI, artificial general intelligence. Even at this late date, formal constraints on this process, moral or governmental, are virtually non-existent. It is assumed as a matter of faith and taught as dogma that all technical progress is beneficial, especially where it is the product of liberal free market dynamics. But the reality is that most technical advances today are spawned within corporate entities that, with only rudimentary accountability, operate autonomously for their own instrumental ends, which often conflict with human aspirations for peace and happiness in a flourishing world.

With the rise of AI, "the definition of the human role, human aspiration, and human fulfilment will change," Kissinger, Schmidt, and Huttenlocher predict in *The Age of AI*,

> What human qualities will this age celebrate? What will its guiding principles be? To the two traditional ways by which people have known the world, faith and reason, AI adds a third. This shift will test—and, in some instances, transform—our core assumptions about the world and our place in it. Reason not only revolutionized the sciences, it also altered our social lives, our arts, and our faith. Under its scrutiny, the hierarchy of feudalism fell, and democracy the idea that reasoning people should direct their own governance, rose. Now AI will again test the principles upon which our self-understanding rests.[188]

If human reason no longer defines the full extent of intelligent attempts to define and understand reality, then a renewed focus on other, distinctly human, ways of knowing would seem to be in order. That would mean a return to value not as opposed to but in concert with, material fact as a tool for identifying authentic worth, and as a corollary, recognizing and fostering *authentic* progress. That in turn involves recognizing the validity of moral realism and the real existence of good, as discussed in the opening chapters of this book.

The challenge is to bridge the gap between modernity's version of progress and a more humane definition in a way that does not stifle positive technical development and its beneficial products, while at the same time defending core human moral aspirations in their application. At this inflection point in our history as a species, we can take some comfort in the fact that we have the latent wisdom and the social and technical resources necessary to steer developments in the right direction. Where the convictions of faith are absent in this increasingly secular world, moral realism can give each of us the courage to act on our best impulses, to do what we know to be right, and to combat what we know to be wrong. And at the same time, to understand the obligation each of

---

188 Kissinger et al., *The Age of AI*, 181.

us bears to take up the moral conversation for too long marginalized in Western modernity.

Trends, both current and historic, will need to be reversed. We will need more, not less, public participation in the processes of democracy; more, not less, thoughtful engagement with established religion; more, not less education in the humanities as opposed to science, math, and technology; more, not less, responsible regulation of our media enterprises to help limit the circulation of deliberate falsehood and incitements to hatred; more, not less, control over the gargantuan business corporations that rule over so many aspects of our lives. And we urgently need international cooperation in drafting the equivalent for AI to the strategic arms limitation treaties of the 1990s which are designed to control nuclear arms. AI's impact on warfare, from propaganda to cyber-attacks on infrastructure, from strategic planning and tactical operations to autonomous battlefield killing machines is beyond the scope of this volume.[189] It will undoubtedly be transformative, and unpredictable, as nuclear-capable super-intelligences aim to outsmart one another at speeds and levels of complexity unavailable to humans.

As we've seen, the kind of paradigm shift called for has happened before, and it can happen again. History has shown it never pays to bet against humanity.

189 Kissinger et al., *The Age of AI,* Ch. 5.

Epilogue

Four hundred years on from the Enlightenment, it is worth remembering that behind their respective structures of power and influence, science and organized religion have, at their best, similar if not identical agendas. Both are interested in uncovering and disseminating the truth about what is real. Their approaches to discovery, though they may appear at first glance to be radically different, are in many ways remarkably similar.

Organized religions, it is true, have arrived at certain firm convictions that they regard as unarguable (including the existence of God the Creator, the possibility of the miraculous, the authenticity of various prophets and teachers, etc.), and which appear to be antithetical to science. Science, for its part, claims to be open-ended and endlessly curious, and is confident that it will, one day, have objectively verifiable answers to any and all questions about the world, including those, like the origins of the universe and life, to which religion has provided explanations that science regards as nothing more than folklore.

The apparent conflict arises out of the fact that science is focused on what it regards as fact—objective knowledge of the properties and operations of the material world—while religions are mainly concerned with value and meaning in the world. Religious "truth" centres on meaning; the issue of meaning (in the religious sense of transcendent significance) is explicitly *excluded* from scientific enquiry because it is not measurable or computable.

The contradiction in the two approaches to truth is more apparent than real, though, because for us humans there is no such thing as knowledge of the physical that is not inevitably entangled with meaning. Science studies the world by reducing it to ever-smaller component parts and collecting meticulously detailed data on each bit and piece, but it makes progress when it is able to reassemble those bits and pieces—those data points—into a whole and recognize the whole for what it *is*. What it *is,* is its meaning. The figurative cogs and wheels of any apparatus take on collective meaning when they are assembled and the purpose of the machine becomes evident. The meaning of a wall clock is time as regulator; the meaning of a washing machine is cleanliness as virtue; in each case there are further levels of meaning we're all familiar with. As any object or biological entity is dissected in the laboratory, it sheds meaning at every stage of disassembly, until what is left is a collection of component parts, each of which is more or less meaningless on its own. The assembled whole is greater than the sum of its parts precisely because of the emergence of meaning. This insight can be observed on the scale of our own world, but it is also relevant to the entire cosmos.

The great defect of science as it came to be practised in the twilight of religious authority in Europe is its refusal to accept that the knowledge it provides is incomplete, and for that reason potentially endangering. To rely solely on its guidance can be likened to setting sail in a wooden caravel without understanding weather, or that the world is round. Of course, the same charge of wilful blindness might have been made against medieval religious authority, which in its rigid moral and doctrinal certainties sank to brutal persecution of scientific explorers and heterodox believers alike.

Critical moral realism as we've been discussing it in preceding chapters offers one way to reunite moral and scientific knowledge—value and fact—acknowledging their inevitable entanglement without engaging in religious discourse. Another approach is its mirror image, as set forth in what has been called critical theology, or theological critical realism. Deeply influenced by the philosophical writings of Michael Polanyi, critical theology applies critical realism to theology,

> … as a way of describing the process of "knowing" that acknowledges the *reality of the thing known, as something other than the knower* (hence "realism"),

> while fully acknowledging that the only access we have to this reality lies along the spiralling path of *appropriate dialogue or conversation between the knower and the thing known* (hence "critical").[190]

The first part of this definition is clear enough: it acknowledges the real existence of things external to ourselves. In other words, there is a mind-independent world out there that is knowable through reason and hence through science. It is not simply a figment of our imaginations. The second part speaks to the idea that, even though we are rational beings, we can only ever approach, and never arrive at, complete knowledge of that world because, as science now acknowledges (if only reluctantly,) there are limits to reason as a vehicle for truly comprehensive knowledge and understanding.

The way to transcend those limits to rational comprehension is through the spiralling path of continuing conversation between the knower and the thing known—making ever better, more complete representations. This path can take many forms, from scientific experiments to prayer and meditation. The important thing is that it is always open-ended, its conclusions provisional. The body of "fact" it produces can be based on nothing more than consensus, whether it involves the properties of sub-atomic particles or the interpretation of sacred texts or miraculous events. For that reason, it is vitally important for the "conversation" to be as inclusive as possible, and for it to focus on both aspects of the real—both fact and value, both the thing known and its *meaning*.

In the modern world, as it has evolved from the time of Galileo, Bacon, and Newton onward, that means reconnecting, in dialogue, the disciplined learning of science and a critical realism focused on value. It means, in other words, re-combining natural and moral philosophy in a holistic approach to knowledge and understanding.

Knowledge that cannot be communicated directly by conventional oral or written discourse is often represented in works of art, in myth, or parables, and in meaningful ritual. In each case, the symbol refers to a reality, and it invites the mind to seek for further evidence and clarification of that reality. A service celebrated in a great cathedral involves many

190 N.T. Wright, *The New Testament and the People of God: Christian Origins and the Question of God* (Philadelphia: Penn, Fortress Press, 1992), 35. Others in this widening community include John Polkinghorne, Ian Barbour, and Arthur Peacocke, all scientists who have seriously engaged with theology. The sociologist Gregory Baum is another.

layers of symbolism intended to convey meaning in their combined expression. That meaning points back to the things, persons, and events being symbolically portrayed, and whatever power the ceremony may have to move people is derived from its deep connection with what is real. This kind of symbolically transmitted truth generally needs to be met half-way, as it were. One must be amenable to its possibility in order to experience it when in its presence. For that reason, spiritual ritual is often designed explicitly to pave the way, to open (or empty) the mind, to prepare it for insight to come.

Michael Polanyi writes that,

> ... the book of Genesis and its great pictorial illustrations, like the frescoes of Michelangelo, remain a far more intelligent account of the nature and origin of the universe than the representation of the world as a chance collection of atoms. For the biblical cosmology continues to express, however inadequately, the significance of the fact that the world exists and that man has emerged from it, while the scientific picture denies any meaning to the world and indeed ignores all our most vital experience of this world.

The role of religious learning is to discover meaning, which need not be incompatible with the truth of science. Religious faith (and in Polanyi's case, Christian faith) represents "an eternal, never-to-be consummated hunch, a heuristic vision."[191] As with any hunch, our natural curiosity demands our continued exploration and clarification, which takes place through a process known, somewhat unappealingly to the twenty-first-century mind, as worship.

Once again it's worth noting the congruency here with the acquiring of scientific knowledge. Science as we know it is possible if and only if its practitioners maintain a faith in the unprovable hypothesis that there is an objective reality that is accessible to us through reason and its tools. It is a faith that is deeply conditioned through long education within highly disciplined institutions. In doing science, we meet nature half-way and proceed from there. In the end, truth—any truth—can only be thought of by believing it.[192]

---

191 Polanyi, *Personal Knowledge*, 281, 199.

192 Ibid. 305.

Both science and organized religion serve the crucial purpose of providing a framework for understanding, a means of resolving into a sensible pattern the myriad of scattered data points encountered in daily living. As the philosopher George Santayana said, it is as impossible to be religious without having a religion as it is to speak language without having a language.[193] In both cases the formalisms of grammar and syntax and the context they provide are essential to comprehension.

Let us accept, for the moment, the contention that without the gifts of science over the past four hundred years, the world would be a more dangerous, unpleasant, and less happy place for its human inhabitants than it is today. (We will ignore the condition of non-human inhabitants, including those raised for human consumption.) Could the same assertion be made about organized religion? Has it, can it, make the world a better place?

First, to state the obvious, all the great religious prophets, from Moses to Mohammed to Jesus to Buddha to Confucius, were pointing to a world beyond, to a world that reveals itself as a moral universe. It could be argued that reason does that too, that an atheistic humanism, the acme of rationalist social philosophy, may well share the same perspective. In fact, the critical moral realism that is at the heart of this book comes to the same ultimate conclusion, or rather, accepts the same basic premise, of a moral universe. However, most people understand humanism to be synonymous with moral relativism moderated by tolerance. Belief, in the sense of faith, is not part of the vocabulary. Atheistic humanism, in other words, is unwilling to take the leap necessary to attaining truth in its most profound and unshakable expression. Without that final step, the moral precepts of humanist society are subject to modification and erasure by shifting political and ideological currents, as the twentieth century demonstrated so tragically.

While organized religion may no longer play much of a direct, operational role in modern society, it could be argued that in its implacable faith in the truth of goodness, it still serves to direct the forward motion in history. Which is a more helpful understanding of "progress" than reason supplies (i.e., technical innovation and growth).

The utopia imagined in religion, whether it be the Christian Heaven, or the Islamic Jannah, or the Hindu Swarga Loka, is not properly thought

---

193 Michael Polanyi and Harry Prosch, *Meaning* (Chicago: University of Chicago Press, 1975), 179.

of as prediction, nor a template to be employed in the construction and management of current society. It is best seen as a reference point that offers a continuing critique of the contemporary world of human affairs, a critique of our secular utopias. In the case of Christianity, the messianic prophecy of the eventual establishment of God's kingdom on Earth is intended to generate "self-actualizing hope (not passive dependence) since the God in whom Christians believe is an enabler and vivifier in history and empowers men and women to act on their own behalf," Baum argues. Further, "faith does not make people inactive; it empowers them to act."[194] Insofar as faith and trust are synonymous, I would argue that trust in the conclusions of moral realism can generate a similar self-actualizing hope in the continuing progress of good.

In the face of dire predictions for humanity and its only habitat coming from all quarters of science and from the humanist arts and letters, and of prospects for technological "solutions" that threaten a hellish future in which humans and robots are blended to produce cyborg automatons, the appropriate message is that the future remains open and undetermined, and we should therefore not lose our nerve.

194 Gregory Baum, *Religion and Alienation: A Theological Reading of Sociology* (Mahwah: Paulist Press, 1975), 284.

Index

Note: Page numbers in this index refer to the print edition of *The Storm of Progress*.

LLP Singles Essays

The Storm of Progress: Climate Change, AI, and the Roots of Our Dangerous Ethical Myopia is the most recent in a series of Singles essays in English and in French by distinguished Canadian writers and translators on a wide range of topics of contemporary interest.

Black Community Resource Centre. *Where They Stood: The Evolution of the Black Anglo Community in Montreal*. LLP, 2023. ISBN: 9781773901343.

Boullata, Issa J. *The Bells of Memory: A Palestinian Boyhood in Jerusalem*. LLP, 2014. ISBN: 9781927535394.

Deguire, Eric. *Communication et violence. Des récits personnels à l'hégémonie américaine*, essai. LLÉ, 2020. ISBN: 9781773900605.

Delvaux, Martine. *Nan Goldin: The Warrior Medusa*, trans. David Homel. LLP, 2017. ISBN: 9781988130552.

Drimonis, Toula. *We, the Others: Allophones, Immigration, and Belonging in Canada*. LLP, 2022. ISBN: 9781773901213.

Farman, Abou. *Clerks of the Passage*. LLP, 2012. ISBN: 9780987831743.

Farman Abou. *Les lieux de passage, essais sur le mouvement et la migration*, trad. Marianne Champagne. LLÉ, 2016. ISBN: 9781988130200.

Fletcher, Raquel. *Who Belongs in Quebec? Identity Politics in a Changing Society*. LLP, 2020. ISBN: 9781927535394.

Gollner, Adam Leith. *Working in the Bathtub; Conversations with the Immortal Dany Laferrière*. LLP 2021. ISBN: 9781773900735.

Henighan, Stephen. *A Green Reef: The Impact of Climate Change*. LLP, 2013. ISBN: 9781927535271.

Homel, David. *How Did I Get Here? A Writer's Education*. LLP, 2023. ISBN: 9781773901404.

Jedwab, Jack. *Counterterrorism and Identities: Canadian Viewpoints*. LLP 2015. ISBN: 9781927535868.

Lavoie, Frédérick. *For Want of a Fir Tree: Ukraine Undone*, trans. Donald Winkler. LLP, 2018. ISBN: 97819881305934.

Michaud, Sara Danièle. *Scar Tissue: Tracing Motherhood*, trans. Katia Grubisic. LLP 2023. ISBN: 9781773901374.

Navarro, Pascale. *Women and Power: The Case for Parity*, trans. David Homel. LLP 2016. ISBN: 9781988130156

Péan, Stanley. *Taximan*, trans. David Homel. LLP 2018. ISBN: 9781988130897.

Rowland, Wade. *Saving the CBC: Balancing Profit and Public Service*. LLP, 2013. ISBN: 9781927535110.

Rowland, Wade. *Canada Lives Here: The Case for Public Broadcasting*. LLP 2015. ISBN: 9781927535820.

Rowland, Wade. *The Storm of Progress: Climate Change, AI, and the Roots of Our Dangerous Ethical Myopia*. LLP 2024. ISBN: 9781773901497.

Salutin, Rick. *Keeping the Public in Public Education*. LLP, 2012. ISBN: 9780987831729.